# Corporate
# Caterpillars

# Corporate Caterpillars

## How to Grow Wings

Ron J. West

iUniverse LLC
Bloomington

# CORPORATE CATERPILLARS
## How to Grow Wings

iUniverse books may be ordered through booksellers or by contacting:

iUniverse LLC
1663 Liberty Drive
Bloomington, IN 47403
www.iuniverse.com
1-800-Authors (1-800-288-4677)

ISBN: 978-1-4759-9402-5 (sc)
ISBN: 978-1-4759-9403-2 (hc)
ISBN: 978-1-4759-9404-9 (ebk)

Library of Congress Control Number: 2013910200

Printed in the United States of America

iUniverse rev. date: 08/14/2013

To my wonderful children, Colin Peter, Claire Louise,
and Laura Catherine, and the lives you inspire.
May we all grow wings.

# Contents

Foreword by Jack Canfield ....................................................... xiii

Acknowledgments ................................................................. xvii

Introduction
*The Journey of Corporate Transformation* ....................... xix
    Committing to Transformation ................................ xxi
    Awareness .............................................................. xxiii
    Getting Real ............................................................ xxiii
    The Bare Necessities ............................................... xxiv
    On Purpose ............................................................. xxv
    A Chunk at a Time ................................................. xxvi
    Removing Obstacles ............................................... xxvii
    Much-Needed Help ................................................ xxvii
    Transformation ...................................................... xxviii

Chapter One
*Awareness: Waking Up from Automatic Habits* .................. 1
    Awareness through Force .......................................... 5
    Awareness through Frustration ................................. 9
    Awareness through Inspiration ............................... 10
    Being Responsible .................................................. 12
    Victimhood ............................................................ 14

Chapter Two
*Getting Real: Seeing the Good, the Bad, and the Ugly* ....... 19
    Finding a Safe Place ............................................... 20
    Attaching a Ritual .................................................. 25
    Getting Real ........................................................... 28
    Behavioral Profiling ............................................... 34

Chapter Three

*The Bare Necessities: Getting beyond Mere Survival* .........40

    The Turning Point...............................................43

    Walk before You Run .......................................48

    A Way of Being.................................................51

    The Need to Shift .............................................54

Chapter Four

*On Purpose: A Sense of Meaning Makes
Everything Easier*...................................................60

    The Ultimate Purpose.......................................62

    How Will You Be? ............................................63

    Your Brand........................................................72

    Mission and Vision ..........................................74

Chapter Five

*A Chunk at a Time: Achieving Uncommon Results*...........80

    Four More Ways ...............................................84

    Rapid Rehearsal ...............................................88

    Plan for the Unexpected...................................90

    Balancing Your Goals.......................................93

Chapter Six

*Removing Obstacles: Overcoming the Inevitable Sabotage* 98

    Change Management.........................................99

    Surprise Surprise .............................................105

    The Unexpected................................................106

    Initiative Fatigue..............................................107

    Not Worth It......................................................108

    The Unconscious Saboteur ..............................109

    Greater Good ....................................................111

    Lacking Intention .............................................113

    Alignment .........................................................115

Chapter Seven
*Much-Needed Help: Vital Support to Get*
*Where You Want to Go*......................................................120
    Accountability..............................................................121
    Masterminding .............................................................124
    Resistance ...................................................................126
    Enrollment ..................................................................128
    Adapting......................................................................131
    You're Fired! ...............................................................136

Chapter Eight
*Transformation: Shifting Your Entire*
*Corporate Culture* ...........................................................139
    Journey of Transformation..........................................140
    Conscious Capitalism ..................................................145
    A Place to Start ...........................................................145
    Are You Ready? ...........................................................147

Bibliography ........................................................................149
About the Author ................................................................153
Index ...................................................................................155

# Illustrations

Figure 1: Quadrant Behavioral Model.................................34
Figure 2: DiSC Quadrants....................................................36
Figure 3: Typical Commercial Real Estate Leader Profile......37
Figure 4: Maslow's Hierarchy of Needs...............................41
Figure 5: Author's Former DiSC Behavioral Profile ..............53
Figure 6: Author's Recent DiSC Behavioral Profile...............54
Figure 7: Be-Do-Have.........................................................67
Figure 8: Example Ways of Being.........................................73
Figure 9: Sample PERT Chart..............................................91
Figure 10: DiSC Profile—Open to Change...........................102
Figure 11: DiSC Profile—Resistant to Change.....................102
Figure 12: Identity—Environment......................................117
Figure 13: Mission—Market...............................................118
Figure 14: Creative Pattern DiSC Profile............................132
Figure 15: Investigator Pattern DiSC Profile ......................133

# Foreword by Jack Canfield

I have had a long and fulfilling career teaching individuals and companies how to get from where they are to where they want to be by applying a time-tested system of success principles that I developed over a 40-year period of study, research, application and teaching to others. Several years ago I realized that if my work were to carry on, I needed to build a team of professional trainers of these success principles to ensure that even more people could learn the principles and apply them to their personal and professional lives. Ron J. West was selected to be one of my very first trainers. When Ron first took the stage to present in front of his peers, I immediately knew he was a natural and gifted trainer. He captivated the group with his presence, his knowledge, and his humor. Over the course of the next year, we became friends and colleagues.

When Ron asked me to write the foreword to this book, I was eager to see what he had written. Again, I was immediately impressed with the power of the writing, the deep wisdom in the ideas, and the easy readability of the manuscript. Ron has captured the essence of what makes businesses and corporations of all sizes grow and become more profitable—the consciousness, awareness and bold actions of the leaders. By sharing his own vast experience in helping turn companies around and growing them, you know that what you are reading is practical and doable. Ron has been there and done that.

We are at a critical time in history where business as usual is no longer an option, and to bring about the changes that are necessary requires a new kind of leadership that requires a personal transformation of the leaders. Ron has mastered how to facilitate that in his consulting work and his own businesses. And now he is sharing these powerful principles and techniques in this book.

At the end of our Train the Trainer program we host a two-hour "Come As You'll Be" party. The idea is that you have to come as the person you will be five years into the future, and you have to dress, act and talk as if all of your goals have been reached and you are living your dream life. Some participants talk excitedly about their new best-selling book. Some brag about their business accomplishments and some bring pictures of their vacation homes, private planes and yachts. Some even recruit friends to follow them in with flash cameras acting as adoring fans and paparazzi. In a spirit of celebration I get to enjoy seeing everyone lock in the experience of their chosen futures as a crucial step in manifesting what it is that he or she truly wants.

One of the first people I encountered when I walked into that particular party was Ron. He was dressed in black tie and tuxedo having just *received an award for his work in transforming corporations.* What struck me about the improvisational conversation we had was Ron's quiet confidence. He immediately impressed me that night, as he still does today, that he truly does have the knowledge, the experience, and the skills to bring transformation and success to whole company cultures.

This book and the ideas within it are a perfect expansion of the success principles that I teach. Ron brilliantly illustrates them with his own compelling business and personal experiences to powerfully show how the growth and development of the leaders in a business bring about the growth and development of the business.

I truly hope that you will have the wisdom and the courage to put into practice what Ron teaches in this book. I also hope you will avail yourself of the opportunity to someday work with Ron in person. You'll find, as I did, that he has a profound gift for facilitating positive and lasting changes in leaders and their companies. When you do, you'll discover, as I did, that Ron and his work are the real deal.

# Acknowledgments

As part of my personal transformation I attended many great workshops. It was at one of those workshops that I had the good fortune to meet Stephen Malone. Since August 2009, Stephen has been my accountability buddy. Stephen not only knows me better than my dear mum but has provided exactly the right feedback at exactly the right time, every time. He has earned my grateful thanks for his unswerving help and support. Without his help the book would simply not have been finished.

I had the honor to study with my great mentor, Jack Canfield, as one of his first personal-transformation trainers. Jack has devoted himself to sharing everything he has learned in the field of modeling success. One of the most important lessons I learned from Jack was that how you are *be*ing has the biggest impact on enabling change around you. We model for each other. Jack has done more for me to model *be*ing than anyone else I have ever met. My heartfelt thanks to you, Jack.

My gratitude is also due to Todd Uterstaedt. Once my executive coach and now my personal friend, Todd has been a very positive and massive influence in my life. So too has Greg Gurnik. His leadership has been an inspiration to me. My personal thanks are also due to Donna Kozik, who encouraged me (and many others) to write a book.

Though I remain responsible for the content of this book and the errors that remain, it would not be at its current stage of presentation without the considerable talents of two exceptional professionals. My thanks are due to Margie Koyak (www.linkedin.com/in/margiekoyak) for converting my draft into readable American English. I am also grateful for the wonderfully creative talents of John Molloy (www.molloydesign.net), who produced all of the illustrations in this book, including the front-cover design and my new website at ronjwest.com.

I am particularly pleased to acknowledge the role that my dear friends Geoff Nicholson and Robert MacPhee have played. Both have contributed directly to my own growth and development. Without their wisdom, their encouragement, and their guidance I would not be where I am on my own journey. You have both earned my eternal gratitude.

A great many people provided valuable feedback and encouragement on this part of the journey, for which I am truly grateful: Brian Acton, Lori Blake, Laurie Schultz, Casey Cupp, Mike Curless, Wil Davis, Sherry Dean, Yvonne Fender, Steve Gandy, Lori Gooding, Cara Grumme, Melina Hill, Oxana Ivashchenko, Dr. Ken Kaye, Amy Kwas, Duane Lakin, Austin Lehr, Flint McNaughton, Tadd Miller, Larry and Jeryl Mitsch, Jim Napoli, Tom O'Brien (sadly, now deceased), Paul O'Conner, Tom Peck, Mike Pellegrino, and Tom Pluss.

I would also like to acknowledge iUniverse for their contribution. Everyone on their team has worked tirelessly and with infinite patience to help publish this book.

I would be remisss in not acknowledging the incredible creative talents of Amanda Reynolds. Her ability to capture the essence of life in her photographic work is exceptional. A sample of her excellent contribution to connecting us all in this tapestry called life is on the back cover of this book (and on my website).

# The Journey of
# Corporate Transformation

> The colossal misunderstanding of our time is the
> assumption that insight will work with people who
> are unmotivated to change. If you want your child,
> spouse, client, or boss to shape up, stay connected
> while changing yourself rather
> than trying to fix them.
> —Edwin H. Friedman,
> *A Failure of Nerve: Leadership in the Age
> of the Quick Fix*

This book does not profess to make the business of business easy. It is not modeled on a single analogy like the transformation from caterpillar to butterfly, nor does it reduce the concept to a set of simple steps. What it does strive to do is to recognize the richness of reasons why we often seem to be left with few choices. This book shows how to move from a world of limited options to a realm of *limitless possibilities*, whether for an individual or for an enterprise. This book is designed to inspire. It provides a kind of "blueprint" you can use to create your own individual and corporate transformation to move from limited to limitless.

Everything shows up exactly when it is supposed to. You are holding this book perhaps because you feel that either you or your company is stuck in some way. As an individual, maybe you have caught yourself repeating a pattern to sabotage your efforts to get to where you want to be. Perhaps you are a CEO, CFO, president, vice president, department manager, or project leader. Probably you are a business leader in a position to effect change in your organization; maybe your enterprise is a small family business or an international conglomerate. It matters not whether your company is a for-profit or a not-for-profit, a public or a private enterprise, this book will help you transform both you and your company.

There are three reasons for this book. A long time ago, a professor at Brunel University in London surveyed a master of science dissertation with some consternation. How could someone who had studied computer technology, software engineering, and microelectronics for so long come to the conclusion that it was not about the technology? The dissertation demonstrated that the only way to build ultra-reliable electronic protection systems was to recognize and address the fact that flawed humans are involved. The dissertation was mine, and the insight developed within it has greatly informed my career as a successful business leader. Instead of repeating the same lessons over and over, as often happens, each experience built on the previous to build a deep knowledge of how corporate change is accomplished. But it stayed true to the theme of corporate transformation: the growth and development of the people *in* a business to bring about the growth and development *of* the business. And so, the first inspiration behind this book is more than twenty-five years of experience driving growth and development.

The second inspiration for the book is my own endless search for an answer. A long-held belief that knowing more and understanding more would somehow provide all the needed love and safety drove my need to read. I avidly studied everything from management, leadership, and change management to psychology and brain chemistry. Reading over nine hundred books has served only to demonstrate the futility of trying to understand everything. Of course, there is no single answer, as the solution lies in the search itself.

For the longest time, life for me felt inauthentic, without meaning or direction. Personal transformation came from numerous self-improvement workshops and trainings. The student was certainly ready, and many great teachers appeared, including Jack Canfield, Deepak Chopra, Dr. Joe Dispenza, Byron Katie, Eckhart Tolle, Dr. Dale Townsend, Marianne Williamson, and Jim Zarvos. Fifteen years of work culminated in graduating as one of Jack Canfield's first personal-transformation trainers.

The third inspiration for the book comes from a realization that a business is a living, breathing, constantly changing entity made up of its collective experiences, memories, hopes, and aspirations for the future . . . much like a person. And, like a person, a corporation can get mired in its past, its perceived limitations, and the reputation it has made for itself, whether good or bad. This realization has enabled me to help many organizations turn their fortunes around by helping them reinvent themselves and putting them on the path to true corporate transformation.

### Committing to Transformation

I believe that many business leaders jump to the fix. They come across a particular methodology and start applying it. Maybe it is because we intuitively know that we need such help to overcome a limitation, or maybe it is needed just to keep up with the competition. The thing is, unless we have a real understanding of our errant habit, the fix typically provides limited results.

It is really *not* about a specific technique. This idea is wonderfully explained in *Failure of Nerve—Leadership in the Age of the Quick Fix* (Friedman 1999, 12). The book's insights into leadership will help you understand at a deep level that our obsession with data and technique is no more than an addiction. It is important to recognize that there is *no single, right technique.* As long as you are committed to change and willing to perform the work, it will inevitably take to effect a change . . . you can and will succeed. It is all about the journey itself.

I should explain that I intend to make reference to certain books that have had a significant effect on my own journey. Though every sample of someone else's journey affected my own, I will share only those books that made the greatest impact. *Failure of Nerve* was one of those. If it is courage you seek to sustain you though transformation, you might find Friedman's book helpful.

This book contains many real, concrete examples from my life, both as a respected business consultant effecting change on a corporate level and as an individual struggling to figure out his own strengths, motivations, and limitations as he makes his way in the world. The examples are *not* intended to be seen as the answer. Every situation is unique. They are merely provided to help ensure you are asking the right questions.

Corporate change is most effective when the leaders of the company themselves embrace change as a way of altering the trajectory of their company. By combining business experience, deep knowledge of the transformation field, and a track record of personal growth and development, *Corporate Caterpillars* gives business leaders like you real insight into their own personal growth and development. It then goes a step further, showing how to apply those same insights as a tool to help your company grow and develop into the success story you want it to be.

## Awareness

Chapter 1, "Awareness," introduces the all-important first step of the journey—to develop awareness. Awareness is a kind of unfolding. Essentially it is the process of waking up from automatic habits. I will use the learning process and a few real-world examples from my own experience to show how and why we develop these habits and how to become aware of them. In my experience, there are three ways to evoke this transition into an aware state. The first is through force. This might be a personal health condition or perhaps a cash crisis for a corporation. The second is through sheer frustration. The status quo is no longer tolerable. The third way to develop awareness is by being inspired to drive large-scale change.

The first thing that most individuals or companies become aware of is that they feel victimized. Someone or something is responsible for their condition. It is vital to break through from being a victim to assuming responsibility. In order to begin to transform, a person must learn to take full responsibility for his or her actions. This is not to say that you are to blame, but once you assume responsibility for everything that happens to you, you are free to take action to change.

## Getting Real

Many times a company forms a quick opinion about a competitor. Then, perhaps to avoid facing pain or embarrassment, the company ignores the fact that its competitor has changed and is now the leader in a segment of the market. It is almost as if we form a view in order to pigeonhole a competitor, preferring to put them down or dismiss them rather than take them seriously and keep a closer eye on what they are doing. All too often, by the time we let it sink in that the competitor is now a very serious threat, it is too late. We ignore the signs of what is really happening.

Chapter 2, "Getting Real," is all about getting honest. And getting real can be tough. We move from victimhood to being responsible by developing awareness. But to get real, we need to find a way to sustain our fleeting awareness. It is achieved by finding a safe place where we can be vulnerable. Typically, someone else models vulnerability for you. Have you noticed that when someone else shares a personal story, you feel closer to that person and are much more likely to open up a little yourself? To be able to get back to this state and so preserve our awareness requires some form of ritual. We tend to build associations to cope with everything, and a ritual is a great way to restore a state or way of *be*ing.

Our reality shifts as we make inquiries. It is the process of inquiry that helps us achieve a realistic view of our situation. We start to see our automatic and hidden habits, beliefs, and attitudes so we can consider making changes consciously.

### *The Bare Necessities*

Once we have a more realistic view of our situation, we often find dysfunction. Let us start with a corporate example. LOFTON was a company that had developed a good reputation for providing software services for over twenty-five years. As their new interim president, I was introduced to an array of new initiatives. Each was presented as the new product that would forever change the fortunes of the company. There was nothing wrong with these product and service ideas in their own right. However, they needed resources that were in short supply, would potentially take a long time to complete, and had at least an uncertain outcome. The company, on the other hand, was almost completely out of cash and in desperate need of a turnaround. Once the owners of the company had a more realistic view of the situation, it was evident to them that the business was not viable in its current form.

I have attended many advanced personal-transformation workshops. All of them had similar rules. You should not attend if you were undergoing therapy, using drugs, or suffering from any type of mental illness. In every case, there were individuals present who were not really "ready" for the trainings. They were not even functional. They were unable to provide for themselves. They saw the trainings as a way to skip a few rungs of the ladder of success. In any event, they needed a form of turnaround to get to a basic functioning level in the world. Chapter 3, "The Bare Necessities," covers the process of building this essential foundation, which is so often skipped.

## On Purpose

The mission and vision of a company is all too often something that is framed, hung on the wall, and then promptly ignored. Many individuals do not have one for themselves. Chapter 4, "On Purpose," shows why the conversation about your own or your company's vision and mission is actually far more important than the final vision and mission statements themselves. Why? Because it is the process that enables different voices from within the company to share their ideas about where the company could be going that is most important.

Okay, so now you know where you want to go. But is it realistic to think you can get there? How will you do it? And what is important to you along the way? Chapter 4 goes on to help readers understand that they must clearly identify who they are and what they stand for, both on a personal and a corporate level—their values—as an essential step toward developing a strong, identifiable brand.

## A Chunk at a Time

Are we there yet? This oft-repeated phrase is all too familiar to parents traveling with small children. And unfortunately, it often applies only too well to our perception of the length of time it takes to achieve our goals and dreams. One of the principles taught in the world of personal transformation is to take your dreams and divide (chunk) them down into more manageable, bite-sized pieces. This translates well to the corporate world. Readers of chapter 5, "A Chunk at a Time," will learn how to make their goals more achievable by dividing them into smaller pieces, establishing phases with realistic time frames, and grouping related tasks together. This may be called the science of goal setting.

The art of goal setting is the addition of emotion to turn each goal into an intention. There is an exercise in many experiential workshops to show the power of such intention. One person is sitting on a chair. The facilitator has everyone focus on trees and roots and heavy metal objects. Then four more people attempt to lift the chair, each with only two fingers on each hand touching the underside of the chair. It can only be lifted a small distance above the floor. Next the participants are asked to imagine feathers and balloons and other light objects. Invariably the chair and the person on it are lifted high into the air and with ease. Try it—it is wild how well this works. It is by establishing a clear target and supporting it with specific intentions that any goal can be reached.

## Removing Obstacles

What are your limiting beliefs, and how are they holding back the growth and development of your company? In other words, what's sabotaging your desire to change? Chapter 6, "Removing Obstacles," will show readers how to identify their own and their companies' limiting beliefs, attitudes, and habits and explains how shining a light on these roadblocks is the way to make them disappear.

While I was growing up, my parents and five siblings taught me the benefits of planning. I became very good at planning everything. I went on to develop a belief that unless things turned out exactly the way I had planned them, I would have somehow failed. So I planned everything and went on to develop strong influencing skills to have things come out the way I had planned them. This worked well for me in my career. Many years later, I realized that it did not work for me in relationships. I was very controlling. Being so strongly attached to an outcome became an obstacle to the success of my relationships. It may be obvious, but it is true that what works on a personal level may not necessarily work on a corporate level—some habits serve at work but not at home.

## Much-Needed Help

No man or woman is an island. In the world of personal transformation, there are many terms used to describe the people in your life who can help you stay on track toward meeting your goals—including *coach, accountability partner, mentor,* and *mastermind group*. Whether it is a single person or an entire group, these types of support systems are critical, as they will help you stay focused, honest, and creative as you travel your path to enlightenment. Chapter 7, "Much-Needed Help," tasks readers to identify the individuals in their lives who could be recruited to play these roles for them. The chapter will also provide specific guidelines to help ensure that the support network created can work as a catalyst for real growth and change.

## Transformation

People like to help others. It gives them a feeling of satisfaction and a sense of well-being and connection. Companies that realize the value of contributing to their community or industry, either as individuals or as a corporate entity, are often leaders within their industry. Is this a coincidence? What comes first, the culture of giving or the industry leadership? Chapter 8, "Transformation," explores the connection between the transformational process of volunteerism and charitable giving on a personal level and shows how companies that tap into the positive effects of this phenomenon by making giving part of their corporate culture can reach new levels in their own growth and development. In fact, the respect these companies earn by "doing good" helps explain why *CRO* magazine's "100 Best Corporate Citizens" list has become regarded as the third most influential corporate ranking list, behind *Fortune* magazine's "Most Admired Companies" and "100 Best Companies to Work For."

As individuals, it feels good to solve problems for others, to be "the good guy," to share our expertise. Quite simply, it's rewarding to be a true leader. Again, this insight in the field of personal transformation is something that can be effectively translated to the business world . . . and is in fact the final step toward becoming a fully transformed company. Becoming an industry leader means looking outside the narrow realm of our own success and profitability to seek out ways to benefit an entire industry or market segment. But it takes courage to become this kind of leader. After all, it means sharing, rather than jealously guarding, some of our best ideas. It means encouraging, rather than stifling, competition. To reach this level of enlightenment, we must learn to operate from a position of confidence rather than a place of fear. Readers of this and the other chapters in this book will gain guidance on just how to grow wings—to transform. And that . . . is our true purpose.

## Chapter One

# Awareness: Waking Up from Automatic Habits

To know others is wisdom;
To know yourself is enlightenment;
To master others requires force;
To master yourself requires true strength.
—Lao-tzu, *Tao Te Ching*

Perhaps you believe your boss is incompetent and you are quite sure you could do a better job of running things. Maybe it is your own enterprise that seems to be stuck. Perhaps you would like to grow your business or take it in a completely new direction. Or you may have started something more grandiose like a personal quest to discover and live your truth. Perhaps you recognize it as a hero's journey. On the other hand, it could seem more like a sacred pilgrimage to you. You may simply think of this journey we are embarking on as a way to make some much-needed changes at work. However you view this journey, the very first step in any such undertaking is to develop awareness.

What is awareness? Awareness is a kind of unfolding akin to waking up. It is experiencing things in new and perhaps very different ways.

What we are waking up from are the unconscious habits we have formed. Driving is a simple analogy. For many people, learning to drive seems overwhelming at first. There are many things to think about in order to safely drive the car. Most people are keenly aware of these things when first learning to drive. We fasten our seatbelts, check our mirrors, pay careful attention to other drivers, and watch out for potential hazards. With new learning and practice we are able to perform most basic driving tasks in an automated way. Many of us more-experienced drivers have had the experience of arriving at our destination with little memory of the journey we took to get there. Once something has been practiced enough it is largely unconscious. It becomes a habit. In effect, tasks that we can perform from habit free our conscious minds to focus on other matters.

Corporations, like individuals, develop their own habits. By way of example, even if a process is not well defined and documented, most companies have accepted ways of doing things. If someone leaves an organization, that person's replacement invariably figures things out and "fits right in," as we say. To make these habits visible we need to shift them from being automatic (unconscious) to conscious. We need to develop awareness and look at these habits from different viewpoints so we can recognize what is happening automatically and determine if these automatic responses still serve as they once did. We might say that we must first climb out of our unconscious state, or reach a state of awareness, so that, good or bad, we might see things as they really are. Once this state of awareness is achieved, we must learn to preserve that awareness and put it to use.

In chapter 2 we will do just that—in effect, we will learn how to step out of ourselves to get a look at what is "real." But I get ahead of myself. First we must wake up.

In the field of learning, it is theorized that we must go through four stages of awareness to master something new. These four stages are helpful to us as a way of explaining why and how we form habits and where awareness fits into our journey. The stages are

- unconsciously incompetent,
- consciously incompetent,
- consciously competent, and
- unconsciously competent.

The first stage is *unconsciously incompetent* or "We do not know what we do not know." I recall when INSOL acquired MICON from one of the mighty conglomerates. INSOL insisted that we simply extract the MICON business unit from the larger conglomerate and move it elsewhere. We were given less than sixty days and little more than our memories to use as a blueprint to complete the move. We found a suitable location and completed the necessary steps to get the new subsidiary started. INSOL was a public company based in London, and the new subsidiary was a hundred-person design and manufacturing firm in the United States. Neither INSOL nor the subsidiary had any prior experience with mergers and acquisitions. This became painfully obvious when, on the day the new subsidiary started operations, some bright spark (maybe it was the intern) asked how he was going to pay for the coffee he was sent to buy. Something as simple and necessary as having a bank account had been overlooked. We were unconsciously incompetent. It sounds foolish (and perhaps even a bit scary), but there are times when you really do not know what you do not know.

The second stage of learning is to become *consciously incompetent*, or "I now know what I do not know." LOFTON is a commercial real estate developer. As their senior vice president of change management, my role was to help orchestrate their growth and development. In just three years, construction volume grew by almost 1,000 percent, twelve regional offices were opened, and the staff expanded from eighty to over four hundred.

LOFTON had spent almost thirty years in the business of developing and building predominantly industrial and office buildings. When the company first seriously ventured into retail real estate, the level of frustration was huge until the whole leadership team realized that things are done differently in retail. Not wrong, just different. While the team was still not aware of exactly what had to be different, they understood clearly that, in order to be successful in retail, there would need to be some new learning. The habits and unconscious behaviors that were successful in industrial and office development did not produce the same results in the retail sector. They were now very much aware of what they did not know.

The third stage is called *consciously competent* or, "You know what you know when you remind yourself you know it." WIZARD was a cable test equipment provider. The company experienced huge demand as cable TV companies converted to digital and added Internet, phone, and digital TV to their service offerings. My role with the company was to completely transform the engineering department in WIZARD at a time when they were a year late with their latest software product and in total overload. In order to meet the demand and calm the chaos, every project had to go through an excruciating process to ensure that every milestone was being achieved and every "i" dotted and every "t" crossed. To implement the new process, a particular brand of project manager was hired from the large engineering contractors nearby that served the military. The new project managers constantly bullied and cajoled the design and development engineers to follow the process. This particular lesson in project management was the cornerstone of what became a huge success.

The final stage of learning is *unconsciously competent*, or "You know what you know without thinking about it." It sounds a little scary, but this is really the only way to handle the sheer volume and complexity of an enterprise. This is also where all the problems begin. To manage the complexity, we move to the stage where we are doing things in an automatic fashion. If the full learning model has been followed, then we have mastered a particular skill and now, through continual use, it has become a habit. Any action repeated becomes automatic. It becomes unconscious. We no longer need to think about how to do that action.

The way that these unconscious habits are learned is innocent enough. A business is faced with a problem or opportunity and finds a method of handling it that seems effective and, hopefully, efficient. The method gets practiced and passed on until it becomes "the way things are done around here." This is a perfectly reasonable way to manage the complexities of running a company, except, of course, when we attempt to use an established habit to handle a different requirement when circumstances have changed.

Before we can replace a habit we must first break it, and before we can break it we must be aware of it. The first step in our transformation journey is to move from *unconsciously incompetent* to *consciously incompetent*. It is to develop awareness. I have identified three ways to develop this awareness—through force, frustration, or inspiration.

### Awareness through Force

One way an individual or a corporation can develop awareness is through what we will label *trauma*. Something happens internally or is caused by external factors that forces a response. I am being intentionally vague here because there are myriad ways that a person or a company can experience trauma and respond. For an individual, it is often a medical condition that prompts awareness and the changes that follow. For a corporation, it might be losing business to a competitor. The common element is that trauma and the resulting response shape the ways things are done from that point on.

A cash crisis is a particularly good way to demonstrate what happens when a business responds to trauma. The inability to meet payroll only has to happen once and most companies (at least those that plan to stay in business) adopt an unwritten rule to ensure that it will never happen again. Some companies have massive cash surpluses that, rather than being used to fuel the growth of the business, are kept in a bank, costing more in lost opportunities than they are earning in interest. This conservative approach could be the response of a CEO who was once scared by a mistyped number on a financial report. Maybe this last example is a little farfetched. Or maybe it's not. Trauma has a way of making an impression. See how this works?

AUTRON was a classic start-up company officially launched by Margaret Thatcher, the former prime minister of the United Kingdom. Founded in an industrial incubator on the grounds of an English university, it used government grants and a little seed capital to develop, at that time, one of the world's fastest computers. On the bright and sunny day that I assumed responsibility as the new CEO, I was a little taken aback when the CFO handed me the keys, wished me luck, and promptly left. I understood that I was taking over to help grow the business.

On my first day with the company, it became apparent that I was left with a staff of twelve and no ways and means to pay salaries. I took a good look at our product. The world had passed it by. With such limited resources, even the ideas for a next-generation processor had missed the window of opportunity. A huge American corporation had spent a long time conducting due diligence with a view to an acquisition. When the acquisition fell through, AUTRON was left without a viable product for sale. It was all but doomed.

The company had been surviving on unauthorized bank debt. In hopes of figuring out how to get out of the mess the company was in, I turned to the consulting work in progress and found an equally sorry story. We had one development project valued at $5,000 and no other near-term prospects.

On my second day, the bailiffs, sent to collect anything of value to offset the company's unpaid electricity bills, visited me. Somehow I managed to convince them that everything was leased and there were no company-owned assets to take. The clock was ticking.

Within a week more vultures appeared in the form of an American distributor who had outlandish plans to distribute the rather specialized computer throughout North America. They explained that, after investing over $1 million in marketing, they had only managed to sell a handful of the computers. Per the terms of their copy of our agreement they were entitled to return the stock they had bought the previous year and receive a refund to offset their losses.

I checked our agreement and drew some comfort when I failed to find a return clause. By the time the executive from the American distributor had arrived from the States, I was ready to take him on. I learned fairly quickly that the AUTRON salesman at the time had deftly changed one page of the agreement after the AUTRON executives had signed it to appease the distributor. Of course, the salesman had long left AUTRON, commission check in hand.

My strategy was simple. I spent a week wearing the executive down. In the end, he agreed to allow us to pay him back as and when profits materialized. What else could he do? Anyway, he wanted to go home. It was almost Thanksgiving.

AUTRON had no viable products in which to invest but did have a handful of great engineers. It seemed the most likely option under the circumstances was bankruptcy. However, this was my new job and I had a mortgage and three children to support. Walking away was not an option for me. In many cases of personal and corporate transformation, trauma of any sort is one of the best motivators for change, especially when that trauma creates a situation where choices are few.

If a turnaround was to be possible, AUTRON needed to clearly identify its priorities. In a situation as dire as the one the company was facing, it does not take a genius to find the first priority—survival. A lack of cash will kill a company, so it was critical that we slow the outflow and quickly find a source of cash to keep things afloat while we figured out what to do. One solution to AUTRON's immediate cash flow problem was to approach the company that decided not to purchase AUTRON and ask them to feed consulting work to the fledgling software house. They agreed. Additionally, the bank to which AUTRON was indebted was persuaded that, with a small additional outlay from the bank, they would have a chance of recovering everything that AUTRON had borrowed. A year or so and lots of great engineering work later, the company that had been on the brink of failure was poised to become a well-known and respected software house serving the UK utility companies and others.

## *Awareness through Frustration*

Another way that an individual or a company may develop awareness is through the frustration caused by an unbearable situation. SIPTON was a very long-standing family business and had built up a considerable amount of commercial real estate. The patriarch of the business had grown up in the Great Depression, so his prudent ways ensured there was little debt. The rents, from mostly mom-and-pop retailers, made the business a great cash generator. Financially it was a very successful business indeed. The work environment, however, was unbearable, a situation that manifested as high turnover—over 70 percent of the employees left each year.

On an individual level, an equivalent story of awareness developing from an unbearable situation is a very personal tale. I had had three marriages that ended in divorce and had been engaged a fourth time. All were truly wonderful women who essentially taught me everything I know. I had mastered the art of unconsciously developing relationships. The habits served me well, at least initially. Unfortunately these same habits would not allow me to sustain a relationship much beyond a couple of years. The pain I was causing others (and myself) simply became too much to bear. Something had to change.

In my first attempt to gain awareness, I enrolled in a year-long transformative program, during which I successfully showed up physically and hid out psychologically. Although I knew that the habits I had relied on in the past to forge a new relationship were not adequate to maintain a lasting one, I was not yet ready to become consciously incompetent. A remarkable teacher and mentor, Dr. Dale Townsend, told me not to worry. He would "install" everything I would need when the time was right. He went on to tell me that I had probably not made a single conscious decision my whole life and I would realize this when I was ready and not before. He was right.

It was some time later that I embarked on another transformative program. It was one of many such programs across the world that has achieved remarkable success in transforming individuals' lives. In one of the very first experiential exercises we participated in, we were asked to mill around the fifty or so participants and say one of only three different things:

- I trust you.
- I do not know if I trust you.
- I do not trust you.

It took a little while for me to realize that I did not trust anyone who did not look me directly in the eye. This realization would not have been quite so scary if it was not followed by the realization that my boss at the time always looked away when he spoke to me. Imagine my surprise. I now knew that I didn't trust my boss. That was worrisome, and realizing that I did not have the trusting nature I thought I did was unsettling. Transformation had begun, driven by frustration.

## Awareness through Inspiration

Perhaps the situation you or your business is in is neither traumatic nor frustrating but something more fundamental is occurring that would provoke awareness. Today more than ever corporations do business across political, geographic, cultural, and religious boundaries. If our businesses were to change the way they operate, the whole world would change. Sounds like a tall order, indeed, to change the world. Think about the effect your own company has, though, on the way your employees interact with others in your company, in other locations in your company, in their own communities, in the places they visit, in other companies and the employees in them whom they interact with.

I used to initiate an induction training I conducted by having everyone consider the number of people they influenced with their decisions. It is a worthwhile exercise you might like to do in your head right now. How many people in your organization could be affected by a decision you make? Think about a decision that might also affect the way they conduct themselves at home. Then how many people are affected? How about the people they interact with—subcontractors, other service providers, alliance partners, owners or investors, friends, family, neighbors, or business acquaintances. Now add the number of people that those people in turn affect. Could you imagine a decision that could touch that many lives? Is it treated with the level of reverence and consciousness that a decision with the potential to affect such a great number of people warrants?

Is it possible that what you do and say could impact, either positively or negatively, that many people? Is it possible that you are not always conscious of the impact your comments or decisions could have on that many people? This ripple effect, combined with today's technology, makes the world a much smaller place. More so than at any other time in history, one person's decisions and actions have the potential to affect so many others. Perhaps changing the world is not such a tall order after all. A company that is healthy and doing well by most standards might nonetheless be stuck. Without the influence of force or frustration, the company could develop awareness a third way—through inspiration. Imagine what would happen if individuals and companies were inspired by the changes that would be possible if everyone made decisions while consciously keeping the people affected by those decisions in mind.

The possibility of awareness can be introduced by trauma, by the situation simply being unbearable, or with the hope of bringing positive and lasting change to many. Actually achieving that awareness is not always a clear path. So what is it that stands in our way of awareness? When I was growing up, one of my favorite expressions to use when I knew I had done something wrong was that "a big boy did it and ran away." It seemed to me that this explanation was the best way to avoid another whack around the ears from my mother (who, by the way, turned eighty-seven around the time I wrote this chapter). Mum was fond of this particular form of punishment, due in large part to her short stature coupled with her desire to have me grow up to be all I could be. Of course the big boy never existed, but I believed that having someone else to blame would surely help me avoid the pain associated with being responsible for whatever it was I had done. For the record, this strategy never worked.

### *Being Responsible*

My lesson of course was to *be* responsible. *Be*ing responsible will ensure that you will never be short of options to *do* what must be done to *have* the success you seek. Here's the thing. The results you seek depend on what you are *do*ing. Everything you do in turn depends on how you are *be*ing. This is as true for an individual as a company.

I once attended a personal-transformation training that was almost entirely experiential. All that really means is that you learn largely by experience instead of the more traditional way of listening to a teacher explain something. One exercise seemed simple. Move from one side of the room to the other.

Move in a unique way that was not the same as anyone that went before you. Easy enough, you might think, until you realize that there were more than one hundred people in the room. With some serious creativity more than one hundred people did indeed cross that room in a hundred unique ways and could surely have come up with a hundred more. This exercise clearly demonstrated that there are limitless ways of *do*ing to get the same end result.

You probably know someone who works in a business that he or she defines in a particular way; say, for example, creative. The company may do many of the same things that your company does—a new marketing campaign, geographic expansion, a new product introduction—but may be experiencing more success than your company. Your friend's company is *be*ing more creative in everything they *do*. While the things they are *do*ing may seem the same as your company, the results are different because they are *be*ing different.

So how do we get to shift the way we are *be*ing? Let's face it, you have probably been *be*ing how you are for a long time and nothing much has changed. Frankly, shifting and changing are not easy. Consider the following example: You are driving along, minding your own business, and someone drives straight into the back of your car. Of course you are the victim. The other driver is entirely to blame. There is nothing you could have done. Is that entirely true?

Let's take a closer look. Were you fully aware of the developing situation? Did you drive defensively and slow down in plenty of time? Did you keep your foot on the brakes or even flash your brake lights? Could you have changed lanes if you had noticed the driver behind was distracted? You may be thinking, *Why should I have to do all that?* The answer to that question is that you are responsible for everything that happens to you. Put another way—there is always something you can do.

I had the distinct pleasure of becoming one of Jack Canfield's first personal-transformation trainers. Many people are familiar with Canfield as the coauthor of the popular *Chicken Soup for the Soul* series and the creator of *The Success Principles*. Over a lifetime of study, Canfield has identified all of the tools, tips, and techniques used by successful people to get from where they were to where they wanted to be. Now known as America's number one success coach, Canfield has worked the principles himself to build his own undoubted success. One of the foundations in Jack Canfield's book *The Success Principles* (2005) is to "Take 100% Responsibility."

## *Victimhood*

If we are not responsible for everything that happens to us then we are irresponsible. Every time in my childhood I said that a big boy did it (whatever I did wrong) and ran away, I was *be*ing irresponsible. Essentially we slip into feeling that we have no control over what is happening. Instead we endlessly complain and find others to blame. We are victimized. A victim takes no action. A victim does not need to, as there is always someone else to blame for everything.

Initially, at least, AUTRON was the victim of their potential acquirer's due diligence process. Instead of taking the necessary action to survive, they had put all their energy into blaming the other company. It was not until AUTRON took responsibility for what had happened that any action could be taken to remedy their situation.

The victim stance is actually a strong one. Sounds a little odd, does it not? When a victim blames everyone else, that blaming comes with benefits. A victim gets attention, feels validated, and does not have to take any risks or assume any responsibility. Think about it. If you do not do anything, then you cannot do anything wrong, so you completely avoid the risk of failure. No wonder victimhood has become such a part of our culture.

This state of victimhood goes hand in hand with feelings of entitlement. It is clear many have surrendered their power to others. Our attorneys and psychotherapists may even have helped perpetuate the whole entitlement culture. It seems that if you can find an oppressor, which is someone else to blame, you are at least entitled to sympathy, if not compensation. This way of thinking has contributed to the increasing number of frivolous lawsuits.

Why does it seem so very difficult to climb out of this victim state? Think of victimhood as if it were a box in which we are trapped. The instructions on how to get out of the box are carefully printed on the outside of the box. Despite the enormous amount of time and effort we expend complaining and waiting for someone to rescue us, the benefits keep us trapped. We clearly have a choice. We have control over the thoughts we think, the images we visualize, and the actions we take. Even doing nothing is a choice. Yet without some form of trauma, frustration, or inspiration, we are unlikely to climb out of the box on our own. It is as if we know that something is not quite right, but it is just easier to blame others for our situation than it is to shift our way of thinking and *be* responsible for it.

How can we climb out of the box and shed our victimhood? How are we to give up all our excuses and act as if we are completely responsible for everything that happens to us? After blaming someone or something for events in your own or your company's life, you may have built resentment. In order to release the emotional tie to resentment and assume responsibility, you will need first to forgive. It is important to realize that to forgive is not to forget. It is more a process of letting go. Where the entire culture of a business is stuck in victimhood and has found an oppressor to blame, it is the leaders of the business who must show the way. Leaders must demonstrate by example that they have let go of their resentment and forgiven whoever or whatever was being blamed.

AUTRON blamed their acquirer's due diligence process for their poor state. It was not helpful to AUTRON's turnaround to continue to build resentment toward that company. Indeed, until the acquirer was forgiven for its perceived transgressions, they were certainly not going to provide AUTRON with the work necessary for AUTRON's survival. In fact, until AUTRON let go of blaming and resenting the acquirer, even the possibility of asking them to help improve AUTRON's situation was unthinkable. As their new CEO, I modeled forgiveness in the way I interacted with and talked about the potential acquirer, converting them to an ally.

It is interesting to note that, in general, we complain only about things that we could change. Few complain that gravity restricts our movement. But, more interestingly, we invariably do not complain to those people who could do something to address our complaint. We complain to everyone else! We must climb out of the victimhood box by replacing complaining with specific actions. Rather than complain about AUTRON's failure to people who had no power to change the situation, AUTRON was proactive and asked the potential acquirer to be involved in the revitalization of the company.

Another way out of the box is through expressing gratitude. It is difficult to remain a victim when you are in gratitude for what you have. The thing to do is to contribute to an individual or cause that is less able than you. Contribution quickly shifts your perception of your own condition. Even a company in turnaround has resources it can share with those less fortunate. Donating employees' time to a worthy cause, especially when the company is struggling, has a dramatic and positive effect on the whole business.

We choose to climb out of our box of victimhood by forgiving and releasing resentment, contempt, and anger. We choose to give up our habitual complaining and replace it with requests for help and actions. We choose to express gratitude for what we have and to contribute to those less fortunate. We choose to assume responsibility for everything that happens to us. It is important to understand that taking responsibility is not the same as taking the blame for everything. Responsibility is really two words—*response* and *ability*. We use our ability to respond any way we choose. The point here is that if you assume complete responsibility for whatever happens to you or your company, there will always be something you can do about it.

What does shifting to a state of *being* responsible feel like? It feels uncomfortable, at least at first. It is uncomfortable to be the one to step up and take action or say what needs to be said. It is much safer and familiar to ignore the early warning signs or to join in blaming someone else for problems. *Being* responsible will be unfamiliar. The entire company will work to avoid the discomfort and return to the familiar. So it will take leadership and courage to overcome these barriers to change. It will take focus to ensure that every single time someone (including yourself) starts to blame someone else you stop and say, "In what way am I responsible for what happened?"

With that in mind, it might be helpful to make a few amendments to Lao-tzu's wise words at the opening of this chapter.

*To know your competition is advisable;*
*To know your own business is enlightenment;*
*To master the market requires strength;*
*To master your own business requires new habits;*
*To master new habits needs discipline;*
*To master discipline takes intention;*
*To master intention first know yourself;*
*To know yourself first become aware;*
*To become aware, shift from victim to responsible.*

If our journey will lead us to this thing called enlightenment, then clearly the root appears to be all about mastery of ourselves (be that individually or as an enterprise). Before we can consider mastery of ourselves, we must first "know" ourselves. It is important to appreciate that to "know ourselves" is more a process than a destination. In this process we continually strive to learn new ways to look at things. The new way of looking at things through the eyes of someone who is not a victim but as someone who is responsible for everything you experience tends to be short-lived, because for most people, becoming truly responsible is uncomfortable and unfamiliar. The challenge is to find a way to sustain our awareness and find a way to stay responsible. *Being* responsible enables us to examine our habits, our ways of doing things. We can develop a realistic assessment of what is going on. We can, at last, get real.

## Chapter Two

# Getting Real: Seeing the Good, the Bad, and the Ugly

> The Rabbit sighed. He thought it would be a long
> time before this magic called Real happened to him.
> He longed to become Real, to know what it felt like;
> and yet the idea of growing shabby and losing his
> eyes and whiskers was rather sad. He wished that he
> could become it without these uncomfortable
> things happening to him.
> —Margery Williams, *The Velveteen Rabbit*

*The Velveteen Rabbit*, a children's book written by Margery Williams, first appeared in 1922. It is a story about a stuffed rabbit and his journey to become real. This classic children's story holds a profound message pertinent to the central issues I address in this book. For now, let's just say that becoming real was not a comfortable experience for the Velveteen Rabbit. It is not an easy process for an individual either. And it is most certainly not an easy thing for a corporation.

In the same way that we lie to ourselves to preserve some self-image, many companies do the same. This is most obvious in a corporation when the environment changes but the firm stays in a state of complete denial until it is almost too late. As interim president of AUTRON, I had the difficult task of presenting the real situation to the owner. Imagine the owner's surprise when I was able to prove that had it continued on its path of "business as usual," the company would have faced certain bankruptcy within five weeks. Getting real can hurt.

The equivalent situation for an individual might be the discovery that your lifestyle is literally killing you. Too often we deny what is real about our state of wellness until it is too late to do anything about it. Is it any wonder that we do the same in our companies? It is far less painful in the short term to stay in denial and keep from getting real. But I am getting ahead of myself. Before we can get real about what is going on in our corporate world we need to find a way to develop and sustain our state of awareness. If awareness is the initial awakening, then we are looking to stay wide awake.

Recall that there are principally three reasons we become initially aware. We can move from victimhood to *being* responsible through trauma or by the situation simply being unbearable or perhaps for the greater good of the many. Whichever approach we use to develop awareness often only provides a temporary glimpse of what is real. Recall my own personal attempts to sustain awareness in my personal relationships. Our need to defend ourselves invariably takes over and quickly returns us to our previous state of denial. It is absolutely no different in the world of work. As soon as we get a sneak peek at what is really going on, we quickly run for cover and return to the same patterns of behavior. The challenge is to get aware, stay aware, and use that awareness to get real about what is going on.

### Finding a Safe Place

Let us assume that you have selected a group of leaders. They are now holding each other accountable to practice constant vigilance and remind each other to first assume responsibility. Even if they could avoid slipping into a state of victimhood, their moments of true awareness would still be fleeting. One of the reasons for that is our great need for safety. In all the many experiential personal-transformation programs I have attended, facilitators work hard to establish a place where participants can first feel safe. It must be a place where it is okay to look foolish or say something stupid. In other words, they come to realize that it is acceptable to make a mistake and learn from your mistake in a supportive environment. Feeling safe is key to sustaining a level of awareness.

Unless you feel safe, you will not share your own version of the truth for fear that you will be judged. The pressure of culture on our behavior is huge. It matters not whether that pressure comes from your immediate family, extended family, workgroup, company, neighborhood, religion, or country. Pretty soon no one will speak up, even though all can see that the proverbial emperor is wearing no clothes. The same patterns we construct to automate the behavior of the company (or individual) stop our creativity in its tracks. But unless we can make it safe in our corporation, we will not be able to sustain awareness.

I have spent most of my career as either an independent or a kind of internal consultant. What never ceases to amaze me is the way employees of the hiring company are only too happy to share insights and observations the moment you make it clear their names will not be used. Again, this only works if you first establish the safe environment. The frustrated employees, including executives, cannot wait to share. This is how and why consultants can look so smart so quickly. The answers, as in all things, were already within.

So how can we construct a safe environment so we can maintain a level of awareness? It may be imagined that this process need only be accomplished once, but be assured that it must somehow be refreshed. Our natural state of homeostasis continuously reverts us to our automatic reactions the moment our safety is threatened. Essentially we are unconscious.

An exercise I frequently share with a new leadership group to help them develop sustained awareness is based on recognizing and comparing their driving styles. Why? Because driving a vehicle is one of the things we work hard to completely automate. Everyone has experienced that drive home where you were unaware how you even got there. But our unconscious driving style is a good clue to how we fundamentally live our lives.

To ensure the success of this exercise, we first must establish that the results of the exercise will only be shared in the small group and are to be kept confidential. It is usually necessary to remind participants of this outside of the training. That is often enough to demonstrate that it is a safe environment. Before the exercise is started, I share a personal story about my own driving style. It is important to model the vulnerability that is needed for the process to work. Without the safe environment, the exercise simply would not work.

The leaders are to concentrate on every detail of their driving style and, as much as possible in a reasonable and safe manner, do the exact opposite for a period of time. Subsequently, a participant I'll call Mick spent a week letting every car go ahead of him on every trip to work and back home at the end of the day. You can imagine his default driving style, can't you? Lenny just kept going, driving much more assertively than he ever had before. The result? A great deal of frustration and a recognition of how tough it is to stay conscious of your automatic habits. But the participants get to see what it takes in a very real, hands-on way.

So what has this exercise shown? First, the leaders in the group have vulnerability modeled for them in a way that confirms it is safe to do so. They can then each share their own experiences, often humorously, knowing it is safe to do so. Laughing at our own driving patterns helps us become aware of them in a healthy way. Calibrating our own patterns against those of others helps us get real about them.

The experiential benefit of the exercise extends well beyond driving. Our patterns of behavior show up in everything we do. Watch the way people move, or play games, or even dance. It is a clue to how they live their lives. It is no different for a company. The challenge is to build a safe environment so that we can maintain a state of awareness long enough to recognize the patterns for what they are. Just patterns.

There is another very excellent leadership-development program uniquely facilitated by a company called Allied Ronin (www.alliedronin.com). It is considered by many to be the most unique, intense, and challenging leadership and team-building simulation available anywhere. Everyone acts as a Samurai warrior in an elaborate game. Not unlike your driving style or the way you move or dance, the way you live your life shows up in how you appear as a Samurai warrior.

Like so many other experiential exercises, the safe environment is achieved through increasing levels of sharing personal information and insights. Unlike the driving exercise where one example is usually sufficient, there are a whole series of exercises in the Samurai Game (www.samuraigame. org) where increasing levels of vulnerability are modeled by the facilitator(s). The Samurai Game sends you home the first evening with some very unusual homework. You are to prepare as though you will die in battle the next day. It is a sobering exercise to write final letters to your loved ones, then clean up your residence and your car, and then rather quickly tidy all your affairs. One poor lady was unsure just how far to take things and drove a few hundred miles to say good-bye to her rather shocked son, in person. The exercise certainly helps you achieve vulnerability quickly.

The next day you are to bring an item to discard. The item has to be something that had previously been important to you, the disposal of which would represent a release for you. When I attended the training, each member of the group stood up in turn, shared a very personal story, and then cast the object into the trash. You have to feel pretty safe to go that deep.

A personal example may help you understand the exercise better. At the time of the workshop, I had recently lost my father. One of his personal possessions that found its way to me was a stuffed red dragon. No one knew why it came into his possession. It reminded me of some coaching I received years before where I was asked to pick an animal to represent the voice in my head. I chose a red dragon and called it Sid. In order to get control of my thoughts I had to visualize quieting the dragon any time my internal voice was a critic rather than a coach. For the record, the technique works well for most people.

Much of my internal dialog at the time of the coaching was based around my early childhood. I guess it is the same for many people. It took several months of quieting Sid to reduce the chatter. For me the significance of discarding the red dragon was a final release of my attachment to my past. I no longer wanted to blame my dad or my childhood for choices I was making at the time.

By the time the whole exercise was finished, the entire group was completely open, vulnerable, and trusting. I have seen this highly conscious state sustained for a few weeks after an impactful training. But it does wane. The trick is to be able to tap back into this safe environment easily instead of having to recreate it all over again.

## Attaching a Ritual

In my experience, the best method for reliably recalling the trust established in a small group is to attach the first and subsequent sharing experiences to a ritual. Recall that Jack Canfield is the coauthor of the *Chicken Soup for the Soul* books and the creator of The Success Principles. After initially building a safe environment at his workshops through increasing levels of sharing, Jack uses music and a hugging process to reestablish the environment. Everyone mills around and, against some very specific music and in complete silence, hugs the next available team member. I am not necessarily advocating hugs every morning at your firm—though it would have a massive and positive effect on company morale. But some kind of ritual would work to reestablish the safe environment.

For example, let us imagine that you decide to start with a small group in your company. Your plan is to develop their awareness and have them go on to form other teams and so broaden the awareness ultimately across the whole company. You start by developing a safe environment for the small group. You have them go through a series of sharing exercises of increasing intensity. Each time, you build a simple ritual involving particular music, motivating pictures on a projector, and a series of steps to follow. You do not need a sharing experience as sophisticated as the Samurai Game to develop the safe environment. If it is attached to a memorable ritual, you will not need to repeat the whole sharing process either but merely help everyone to recall the feeling by going through the ritual.

It is important, though, that the same amount of care and attention is paid to the experience of other participants joining later. I have often seen stages skipped as the exercises ripple out across a company. It is not the ritual that creates the safe environment. It is simply a reminder for those who were properly inducted into the space through modeling, sharing, and giving a chance to build their own feeling of safety to be vulnerable.

I once led a substantial reengineering project in a company with several thousand employees. The objective was to find one way of doing things in a new company born of a sequence of mergers and acquisitions. A new brand was developed along with a new mission and vision. Before the reengineering project was launched, a firm of consultants was retained to get everyone aligned.

No real effort was made to celebrate what had happened before in each of the constituent companies. Without at least some period of mourning everyone was left to conclude that nothing that had happened before had any value. Unfortunately this led to some immediate distrust. Over one hundred representatives from the various companies were selected for the one-day "alignment" workshop. Tables of ten to twelve participants started working on solutions to ill-defined problems with barely any introductions. Sadly, at least in my experience, this is more the norm in mergers and acquisitions.

At LOFTON, I used a series of techniques to encourage increasing levels of sharing as part of a servant-leadership initiative. With a small group it was a fairly simple process to create a safe environment. In each group there were always those happy to open up to show the rest that it was safe. Although it sometimes took a few sessions, everyone would reach a level of openness. There was seldom any awkwardness.

In the few instances where an individual had some reluctance to open up, another member of the team would adopt a mentor role. Most often it would happen naturally. The mentor would provide coaching on a one-to-one basis, establishing trust in a more intimate environment first. Typically, after one or two sessions the individual would rejoin their group and be just as open as anyone else in the group.

One very excellent resource that explains an effective way to accomplish this process is *Leadership and Self-Deception* (The Arbinger Institute 2000, 1-180). A new employee is taken through a series of conversations that cause him to reflect. In essence the difference between being unconscious and conscious or, in their parlance, in or out of the box is how you treat people. In the unconscious state, we treat people as objects.

If we are self-absorbed, we are focused on self and so are "in the box." We are unable to think of others or want to work together as a team. We are entirely focused on protecting self. In this state we are most unlikely to want to be real. This is exacerbated when we are in fear. In a state of fear, we feel completely unsafe and so are even less likely to want to get real. We are too busy protecting ourselves. If you think about how stressful life is these days it is no surprise that our adrenal glands get worn out, unable to keep up with being in a state of constant fight or flight.

It is tough to get aware when we are in this state of fear. While we are fearful we tend not to notice how much help is available. We become massively self-absorbed in defending ourselves, unable to judge whether the threat is even real. The corporate equivalent of this is a company in need of turnaround. A company in trouble is typically acting out of fear. Only when the fear subsides can the company begin the process of *being* real and opening up for growth and development.

*Leadership and Self-Deception* does an excellent job of walking through the conversations that very slowly create a safe space. A number of leaders in the sample company each demonstrate vulnerability and model it for the new employee. Each of the leaders provides feedback to build awareness in a character called Tom Callum—the new recruit at the fictional Zagrum Company. Finally, *Leadership and Self-Deception* provides solid examples of how to get and stay conscious to connect to others in empathetic and positive relationships.

It is quite impossible to get real about what is going on with us, either individually or as a company, without these empathetic and positive relationships in place. Using the children's classic *The Velveteen Rabbit* as inspiration, Toni Raiten-D'Antonio (2004) wrote *The Velveteen Principles: A Guide to Becoming Real—Hidden Wisdom from a Children's Classic*. This book does a fabulous job of explaining that these empathetic and positive relationships are the cornerstone of getting real.

### Getting Real

So with a safe environment and a ritual to reestablish the state of awareness both in place, how can we go about using our awareness to get real about what is going on? One of the techniques used in the world of personal transformation is a simple use of inquiry to facilitate a shift in thinking. Sounds pretty obvious, but the results are profound.

Einstein said, "We can't solve problems by using the same kind of thinking we used when we created them." Yet as soon as a new employee joins the firm and questions how something is done, the culture quickly shuts him or her down. I am not talking here about the unconscious desire for someone to attempt to recreate his or her former existence. That happens often enough. I am referring to the conscious inquiry about why something is done a particular way. It is to be encouraged.

In one of my favorite movies, *A Beautiful Mind,* Russell Crowe plays the part of brilliant mathematician John Nash, an English university professor plagued with schizophrenia. He saw, heard, and interacted with a number of imagined characters and could not tell the difference between this imagined world and the real world. It almost destroyed his career. After years of a worsening condition and a series of failed treatments, including electroshock therapy, Nash asked himself a question. His inquiry was simply, "Is everyone in my world aging at the same rate?" The answer was no and enabled him to discern the real people from the imagined characters in his life. He was able to discern the difference and find a way to function, despite the infliction. This true story of Nash's phenomenal mathematical achievements ultimately earned him a Nobel Prize and a place in history. Our goal now is to identify what is real in our company. There are several approaches that we can use to ask ourselves the difficult questions.

Here is a very simple way that inquiry can help us get real about what is going on. Look for words used in the common expressions used in your company that end in *-ed.* A simple exercise in two parts works well for this. Initially ask the group to describe the culture of the company as if they were describing a person. They might say it is disconnected, or depressed, or even trapped.

The way of shifting this thinking is to use "-ing" instead. Next have the participants rework their former statements. "My company is disconnected" can be shifted to "My company is disconnecting from the reality of the marketplace through fear of the unknown." "Our firm seems like it is depressed" can be shifted to "Our company is depressing itself by failing to focus on playing to our strengths instead of being a slave to our weaknesses." "Our corporation is trapped" can be shifted to "Our business is trapping itself by inaction and by believing things which are simply not true." It is a simple but empowering exercise.

A well-known figure from the world of personal transformation has something to teach our corporations. Again, it is through a process of inquiry. Byron Katie's basic premise is that it is not a given problem that causes our suffering but rather our thoughts about it. These are the questions she suggests asking ourselves about things (problems/thoughts/feelings) we believe to be true in what Katie calls "The Work" in her book, *Loving What Is* (2002):

- Is it true?
- Can you absolutely know that it is true?
- Can you see a reason to stop the thought?
- Can you think of a reason to keep the thought?
- How do you react when you think that thought?
- Who would you be without that thought?
- How can your thought be turned around?

You are either attached to these ideas or you are consciously inquiring. If our goal is to get real, then we must question "the way things are done around here." For example, an English company I worked for was one of the world's preeminent safety system providers and had swelled to five hundred employees to generate $40 million in revenues. With plans to go public, we certainly had a need to question how things were done. Every safety system was quite unique. Every design, packaging plan, manual, and training class was custom. It had continually refined the way things were done for over twenty-five years and had never done anything the same way twice. This was typical. The English tend to approach everything as a unique problem. Americans are more often likely to come up with a product that meets most of the needs so they can move to volume.

Was it really true that it took five hundred people to make a system? Was it really true that every system needed to be totally unique? Was it true that it could not be tackled in a more cost-effective way that would meet customers' needs? At the time the engineering contracting profession was going through a metamorphosis itself and challenging the combative way it had tackled projects in the past. This was the oil and gas industry in the early eighties. The idea of collaboration was embraced. Everyone was working to build trust and interdependence. Costs came tumbling down. Savings were shared and work multiplied. It was a time of huge change.

In such an environment, it became the most natural thing in the world to question how everything was being done. The tough questions were being asked. As soon as fellow leaders saw the fallacy of the way things had been done in the past and the possibility of how things could be done in the future, we only had one more hurdle to overcome. The chairman and CEO had never fired anyone. The belief was that firing anyone was an admission of failure on his part. Was that true? Had anything changed that might cause us to rethink?

Another inquiry tool we can use is from the field of quantum linguistics. Essentially we ask about something in four different ways. If we take the same example we would ask:

- What would *happen* if we found a way to *do* the same work with fewer people?
- What would *happen* if we did *not do* the same work with fewer people?
- What would *not happen* if we did *not do* the same work with fewer people?
- What would *not happen* if we found a way to *do* the same work with fewer people?

Let us imagine that our chairman and chief executive answered the first question as follows: "Simplify to reduce errors and improve efficiency to improve profitability." That makes sense. Let us pretend that he answered the second question with "We would lose business to our competitors." And let us take it that he answered the third question as follows: "The business would not grow and would ultimately be left behind in the market." Both of these answers seem to make sense too. But let us assume that the answer he gave to the final question was "We would not have to fire employees and so would not damage our reputation and look bad." This is the incongruence.

The incongruence in the final answer points to the erroneous belief that downsizing would ruin the company's reputation. The technique is helpful in identifying inconsistencies in assumptions. The consequence was clear. The removal of the roadblock resulted in the business expanding its range of products and services, substantially increasing revenues, and at the same time, reducing the headcount to two hundred.

The chairman/CEO of the English company described above was certainly a very dominant individual and was, at first, very resistant. It ultimately made effecting change in this situation easier with only one person to persuade. Once just one person could get real, the initiative took off.

I saw this effect later at one of the world's absolute best leadership-development programs. The Center for Creative Leadership (CCL) is a not-for-profit organization founded more than forty years ago to advance the understanding, practice, and development of leadership for the benefit of society worldwide. The CCL believes that leaders are made, not born, and that they can adapt and change. They believe that strong interpersonal skills, grounded in personal reflection and self-awareness, are the key to effective leadership.

I had an opportunity to attend their leadership-development program and have since recommended it to many other leaders. In essence, the program collects a huge amount of data from your supervisors, peers, and subordinates and throws all of it at you on the first day. It is overwhelming. The desired effect is to crack open your shell and prepare you for change. The balance of the week is spent understanding what all this data means and developing competencies and strategies. The course culminates in a half-day coaching session. By the end of the weeklong course you are all "put back together."

What I witnessed in the program and have seen many times since in my career is the response of highly dominant leaders. They will take feedback only on their own terms. The CCL program is one that is able to open up even the most resistant leaders.

I once failed to win a very interesting assignment for a banking software company because I underestimated the resistance I would encounter. The CEO was a serial entrepreneur. His CFO, my contact Bert, was afraid that the company was simply repeating its "formula" and was in danger of ultimate failure. Bert assured me that the CEO was absolutely ready for change. I did not wait to form my own opinion. As soon as he showed me into his office, I launched into just how much change I could help provoke. He was petrified. I realized quickly but still too late that this man had a tenuous grip on his leadership. A direct threat to his ultimate control was his worst fear.

## *Behavioral Profiling*

Sometime later, I came across a better way of quantifying this leadership effect that has become a way of measuring the same in a whole enterprise. You may have been exposed to the DiSC during your career. DiSC is a quadrant behavioral model based on the work of Dr. William Moulton Marston in *Emotions of Normal People* (1928) to examine the behavior of individuals in their environment or within a specific environment. It focuses on behavioral style.

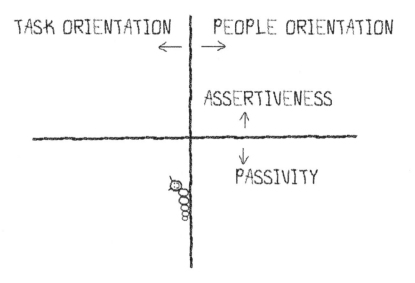

**Figure 1: Quadrant Behavioral Model**

Along the vertical axis is the degree to which you feel you can control your environment. The horizontal axis is used to denote to what degree you believe the environment is friendly. Above the horizontal line it shows degree of assertiveness, while below the horizontal line is level of passivity. The lower down the vertical line your behavioral style is represented, the more passive you are. The left side of the vertical line denotes task orientation. Finally the right of the vertical line records the strength of people orientation.

The resulting four quadrants make up the acronym DiSC. Individuals in a given environment who believe that they have a high degree of control over their environment and with a predominantly task orientation would have high "D" or Dominance scores. Individuals in a given environment who believe that they have a high degree of control over their environment but with a predominantly people orientation would have high "I" or Influence scores.

Individuals in a given environment who believe that they have little or no control over their environment and with a predominantly people orientation would have high "S" or Steadiness scores. Finally, individuals in a given environment who believe they have little or no control over their environment and with a predominantly task orientation would have high "C" or Compliance scores.

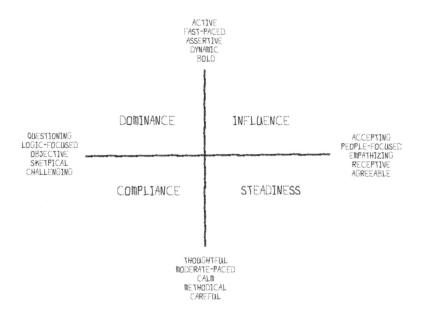

**Figure 2: DiSC Quadrants**

Leaders in the commercial real estate industry, in particular, score high in Dominance and are very active in dealing with problems and challenges. They are typically demanding, forceful, egocentric, strong-willed, driving, determined, ambitious, aggressive, and pioneering. Low D scores describe those who are conservative, low-keyed, cooperative, calculating, undemanding, cautious, mild, agreeable, modest, and peaceful.

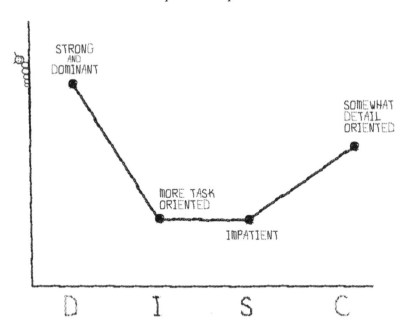

**Figure 3: Typical Commercial Real Estate Leader Profile**

It should come as little surprise that those individuals in positions of authority with a high Dominance score are resistant to developing awareness. What is more of a surprise is that an average score of a workgroup, subsidiary, or even an entire enterprise can show the overall cultural tendencies of a firm. A company with overall high Dominance will demonstrate the same resistance.

For many organizations, the only way to get this kind of inquiry moving is by bringing in outside experts. The right consultant can act as a catalyst. There is another potential trap here, though. Many large and well-established consulting firms have taken to branding their approach as a product.

AUBURN was a pure-play communications test equipment company. Through a sequence of mergers and acquisitions it had positioned itself as number two in a fast-growing segment of the telecommunications industry. With its eyes on the prize of the top slot, the firm set about reengineering its processes across eighty-four countries to build a single company.

On a huge reengineering project for AUBURN I was appalled to discover that in exchange for $1 million, my employer received a deck of PowerPoint slides. If the only tool you have is a hammer then the only problem you will find is a nail. It is the process of inquiry that is paramount. And if the company or one or more influential leaders are dominant, their engagement in the process of inquiry is even more important. Again, whether it is a whole culture that is dominant or a single owner, they must first be enrolled in the process of developing and sustaining awareness and engaged in the process of inquiry to get real.

You may be starting to concern yourself with undoing everything in the firm. I am not advocating that everything be changed. But it is certainly healthy to question everything. So how on earth can we question everything a firm does unconsciously to continue its growth and development and ensure that it is not stuck? In the same way a shaman knows what kind of a challenge to give his or her students or patients to help them on their personal and quite unique path of growth and development. But is there a way to systematize this so we can use one particular approach in quite unique circumstances? The short answer is "no."

One or all of the methods of inquiry described in this chapter can open the door to your reality. They can each or all help you discover what is real about your business. But a word of caution is in order. The drive to understand is an attempt to gain the illusion of mastery. Once we say we understand something we stop thinking about it. Another way to approach things—and I believe a better way—is with awe and wonder. The challenge for corporate healers is to avoid actually believing in their favorite solutions. Every situation at each moment is quite unique. The shamans teach us to hold everything as a mystery. The inquiry works because it is applied in the moment with no predetermined answer. Beware the consultant who has the answer. It is the question that will unblock your path.

Our questions invariably uncover something we have been trying to avoid. Typically we are the last to discover something pretty obvious to everyone else. That something is dysfunction. We are shocked to find that we are not attending to the bare necessities of life.

Chapter Three

# The Bare Necessities:
# Getting beyond Mere Survival

Opportunities to find deeper powers within ourselves
come when life seems most challenging.
—Joseph Campbell, *Pathways to Bliss*

Once the door to reality is opened through inquiry, the first thing we typically discover on the other side is what is broken. With that comes the realization that in order to make any progress we must attend to what is not working. The kinds of challenges I am talking about are elemental needs.

You are probably familiar with Maslow's hierarchy of needs. Though some of the detail of Maslow's work has been called into question, the basic premise stands: as individuals, we must first attend to our physiological needs; they are the literal requirements for human survival. If these requirements are not met, the human body simply cannot continue to function. In the same way, a company without the cash to make salaries must first attend to its survival.

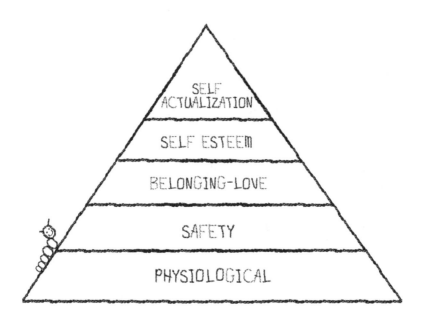

**Figure 4: Maslow's Hierarchy of Needs**

In the same way that the definition of "survival" is different for every individual, it is also unique for a given company. For one individual it might mean being "clean" of addictions and able to perform some form of work. For another it might mean an annual income of $50,000 and a well-established support network. It all depends on what is normal in a given environment. Similarly, for one company "survival" might mean having enough cash to make salaries and cover interest payments and perhaps three months' work in the pipeline. For another, it might mean 8 percent pre-tax profit and two years of contracts. It all depends on what is normal for the industry.

Before a company, or a person, can reach any kind of meaningful turning point in their growth and development, they must first address the mechanics of getting functional.

No more, no less. To get you or your company from where it is now to the turning point it needs to reach requires aim, focus, willpower, and accountability.

**Aim and Focus:** The work of survival must begin with a clear focus on what the turning point will look like. In other words, where do we hope to go?

**Willpower:** Without the willpower to make changes, no recovery will work.

**Accountability:** Willpower alone will not work without a support network and others to hold you or your company accountable.

The realization that something is actually broken and not functional is usually enough to drive individuals and whole businesses back to victimhood. You might see now why it is so very important to build a safe place, as described in chapter 2, and how the way to get back to that safe place is to sustain awareness. As strong as your willpower or intention might be, habits are hard to break.

You will find that there is more willingness to accommodate change when in survival mode. But still, the intention alone is insufficient to achieve a turnaround. I have experienced many examples of plans for change being introduced with PowerPoint slides. And then . . . nothing. It is as though management believes that the conscious intention of a much-needed change will be enough to cause an entire enterprise to forget everything it knows and make a quiet shift to a new way of *being*. But unless the unconscious habits of the company are addressed, there will be no change.

A very popular approach to instituting meaningful change in our lives is captured in *The Secret* (Byrne 2006). Rather than focus on what we do not want, Byrne advises us to place the emphasis on what we do want to attract into our lives. The law of attraction states that you attract into your life whatever you think most about. Your dominant thoughts will find a way to manifest themselves.

However, I have personally witnessed in many separate cases individuals getting clear about what they want and opening themselves up to what they really want . . . and there they stop. Why do so many attempts to change, even when maintaining the status quo is clearly destructive, fail? The key part of *The Secret* often overlooked is the need to do something different to bring about change. The missing piece is the need to take action. It sounds like an oversimplification, but it is as true for an individual as it is for a company. A new habit must be learned to replace the old.

## *The Turning Point*

I learned in many different experiential-training exercises ways of stopping thoughts or feelings. The "stop" process can take many forms. In my case, one of the most effective was to visualize a train loaded with negative or unhelpful thoughts or emotions coming to a complete stop at a wall and instantly dissolving. It worked. This visualization would effectively halt a thought or a feeling that was not serving me in the moment.

The wall represented my block to what came next. However, I realized much later that simply blocking a thought or feeling did not effect lasting change. Something needed to be added—what I *did* want to experience—be it a thought, a feeling, or even an attitude. I've learned that this kind of action is critical to get through survival and reach the turning point.

Maslow's hierarchy of needs demonstrates that a series of needs must be met before anyone can attend to the lofty idea of self-actualization, at least in the North American culture. In a similar way, a company unable to make payroll should not be too concerned with refining its branding. Once basic needs are met, then and only then can we shift to a mode of growth and development. There is a huge turning point between these two states that is often only apparent well after it has been navigated. Taking care of meeting basic needs requires a survival mode. It is exactly the same for a corporation. Turnaround is a very different kind of mode than growth and development. It is important to recognize the differences on either side of the turning point. They require very different ways of *being* to work effectively.

For both individuals and corporations, it is difficult to identify exactly what the turning point will look like. But it is important, nevertheless. After all, it is unhealthy to stay in a mode of recovery for too long. It is likely to do more damage than good. In the case of an individual, the danger is the possibility that you will come to depend on the recovery mechanisms themselves. One addiction is replaced with another. For a company, that translates into staying risk averse and failing to fuel growth when conditions are right. It is stuck in a mere state of preservation.

In the case of AUTRON, the turning point was when the cash flow became positive. What was interesting was the resistance to invest even when there was cash to spend and benefit to be gained.

Part of the required reading for the Turnaround Management Association, an international community of turnaround and corporate renewal professionals, is the *Principles of Corporate Renewal* (Platt 1998). Platt recognizes four precepts of corporate renewal—authority, vision, buy-in, and extension. I have come to realize that Platt's four precepts apply equally well to both personal recovery and corporate turnaround. It is interesting to directly compare personal recovery with the institutional process of corporate turnaround.

|  | **Individual** | **Company** |
| --- | --- | --- |
| **Authority** | Without the willpower to change, there can be no recovery. | It is the same for a company; authority must come from the top. |
| **Vision** | It is vital to define the turning point. | It is the same for a company; what constitutes recovery must be defined. |
| **Buy-in** | Obstacles to change must be eliminated. | It is the same for a company; forces that stand in the way must be neutralized. |
| **Extension** | The process of change can be learned and used to support future growth and development. | The process of change can be learned and used to support future growth and development. |

Another model we can use to think about this process is the twelve-step program. Although originally developed in the 1930s to treat alcoholism, it is now well established as a way of dealing with a wide range of addictive or dysfunctional behaviors. In personal or corporate turnaround, we are focused on more than something that simply blocks our evolution. It is something that results in a dysfunctional behavior. Or maybe even an addiction. This version of the twelve-step program is taken from John Bradshaw's 2005 book *Healing the Shame That Binds You: Recovery Classics Edition.*

In the twelve-step program, the steps are tackled sequentially, and the first three of the twelve steps restore us to a state of reality.

- We admit we are powerless (over whatever the addiction) and our lives have become unmanageable.
- We come to believe that a power greater than ourselves can restore us to sanity.
- We make a decision to turn our will and our lives over to the care of God as we understand God.

The fourth step has us back in relationship with ourselves with the possibility of remedy. This step is akin to beginning the use of inquiry to develop a real picture of our state of health.

- We make a searching and fearless moral inventory of ourselves.

It is all well and good, as an individual or the leader of a company, to "get real" about our condition. But no progress can be made if we do not admit it to others. No action will be taken if it is a private thought alone.

- We admit to God, to ourselves, and to another human being the exact nature of our wrongs.

The next step is all about an act of faith and hope. Essentially we develop faith in the plan for turnaround.

- We are entirely ready to have God remove all these defects of character.

At this step there is an appreciation that we can change. It is a deep realization that change is necessary, and it is possible.

- We humbly ask God to remove our shortcomings.

In all twelve-step programs, the "fix" entails being truly conscious of the harm caused and seeking forgiveness. In this sense, the forgiveness is really a release. Admission of the mistakes made, the will to address them, and taking action are powerful steps in ridding ourselves of addiction or dysfunctional behavior.

- We make a list of all the persons we have harmed and become willing to make amends to them.
- We make direct amends to such people wherever possible, except when to do so would injure them or others.

To ensure that we do not repeat the mistakes of the past, we build in a process to continually "get real."

- We continue to take personal inventory and when we are wrong, promptly admit it.
- We seek through prayer and meditation to improve our conscious contact with God, as we understand God, praying only for knowledge of God's will for us and the power to carry that out.

In the final step of the twelve-step program, we show others that there is hope. For an enterprise, this means sharing our best practices in the service of a whole industry.

- Having had a spiritual awakening as a result of these steps, we try to carry this message to others and to practice these principles in all our affairs.

## *Walk before You Run*

It is important to stress again the very great difference between turnaround and growth; dysfunctional and developing; broken and improving. In the case of both AUTRON and LANDIS there was a very simple relationship between cash position and profitability. With no other balance sheet complexity, until they became profitable, there was insufficient enough cash to meet obligations. In both cases there were no other assets to play with, save selling the time of a group of excellent engineers.

Software engineering service work is paid for on a very short cycle, typically thirty or even fifteen days after the work is performed. Most of the costs are salaries and interest for the debt to the bank that funds the turnaround. Work is very profitable and quickly turned to cash to pay back debt.

Using this approach, once each business was debt-free, thoughts turned to growth. Through knowledge gained from one of its contracts, AUTRON recognized a need for an electronic product, initially designed for London buses to "communicate" with smart signs at bus stops. Development of this product gave the business a growth opportunity that was not simply dependent on the number of engineers hired and the engineering time sold. It quickly quadrupled its revenues and significantly improved profitability.

LANDIS, on the other hand, had very grandiose plans to develop a new software product. It could ensure interoperability between pieces of equipment even though sourced from separate manufacturers. The product was something that would help all these separate pieces of equipment "talk" to each other. The business attempted to use profits to fund this development and took some time to adjust its view of reality.

AUTRON more readily accepted its state and dropped its hopes for a new high-speed computer. They realized that development would require massive funding to stand a chance of success. They had built a company of smart engineers that was viable as a business in its own right.

When I joined SIPTON, there was a request to start a kind of book club to discuss the work of Jim Collins in his 2001 book *Good to Great*. In itself, this was a very excellent idea. But at the time, attrition at SIPTON was north of 70 percent per annum. Every year, more than 70 percent of the employees were either fired or left without notice. There was a huge list of dysfunctional behaviors that needed to be attended to first.

Many readers of Eckert Tolle's 2005 book *A New Earth: Awakening to Your Life's Purpose* are immediately captured by his wonderful invitation to a more spiritual life. I happen to like his work. Though I have to say that I have witnessed many seekers find a teacher, a guru, and use the words learned to demonstrate their spirituality—all while they are unable to pay their bills. It is one thing to make a conscious decision to rid you of material things and live a simple life. It is quite another to claim that you are not materialistic in order to disguise the fact that you are unable to care for yourself. First things must come first. Again . . . recovery is needed before we can turn to growth and development.

In hindsight, it is amusing to note that in the case of both AUTRON and LANDIS I elected to use the identical tool to denote the switch from turnaround to growth. Typically during turnaround, all discretionary expenditure is halted. The first to go is usually any investment in physical facilities. Everyone is more willing to tolerate making do with whatever is available. There were few complaints about the shabby wall covering, the lack of adequate storage space, or the broken drawer on the desk.

However, at both companies, I chose to spend a little money on painting and decorating—some new wall covering, a splash of new paint, one or two pieces of necessary furniture, and some essential repairs. It was the first sign of investment after months of austerity. In both cases, a number of employees offered to help and contributed their own time to make some much-needed improvements. And in both cases, the shift in how people felt was palpable.

Though the controller at the time could not see an immediate payback, the value was clear. There was a huge shift in how employees felt about the company. More than any all-company speech, it was a clear signal that something had changed. Instead of the focus being on getting something working, it had shifted to improving what was already functioning. It was time to make careful investments.

Sometimes it is necessary to mark the switch from recovery to growth in cases of personal transformation too. Like a lot of people I have come to know, money was not talked about in my family, so I personally found it difficult to talk about it too. As a direct consequence, I learned a very important lesson about money at one time in my life. And I only had to learn it once. I built a substantial amount of debt in trying to keep up the pretense of a particular style of life. I spent weekends on the beach in Miami, ate dinner at fine restaurants in Boston and New York, and snow skied on the best slopes in Denver, Colorado. When the fourth credit card maxed out, I realized that I had to do something. A year or so of austerity followed. The day that I knew I had completed dealing with the errant behavior was the same day I decided I could afford to pay cash for a new guitar.

Another change came in the kind of language I was using. I once retired for a whole week to the beaches of Tunisia to read a book. Hey, it was a big book. After reading its some 1,200 pages, I summarized the book thus: you can only have people think differently about things by using a different language set. I started using a different way to talk about money to myself. Instead of saying to myself, *I want to buy this,* I would ask myself, *Can I afford this?*

Typically during a turnaround, I will listen for a phrase that will capture a focus for everyone. In the case of AUTRON, the desperate shortage was cash, so the most often used phrase was "go get the money." It became a kind of war cry we would use to remind everyone when visiting customers to ask for better payment terms, to break projects into deliverable (and chargeable) phases, and to ask for more work and referrals. What is important to note is that this too needs to change once you move from turnaround to growth. New phrases need to be introduced to the culture to help shift the way of thinking at each new stage of your growth and development.

## A Way of Being

In addition to the language used, an enterprise can take cues for its ways of *being* from strong leadership. It takes a very different style of leadership to turn a company around than it does to grow one. One way to appreciate the differences is to consider a case where a corporation knows that it is in trouble. When I first arrived, AUTRON had no ability to pay salaries. Bailiffs were at the door. There were no products ready for sale and no customers established for any services the company might provide. There was a very great need for a very fast response. Any delay would surely give cause to the bank to demand repayment of the debt and force the company into bankruptcy.

In the case of AUTRON, there was no time to carefully analyze the company's situation and involve employees in considering possible options for future sales growth. It was find cash or close. There was little time and frankly little need to persuade. The reason for any wholesale changes was already evident to all. So a less-participative style of leadership was more readily tolerated. At the time, I used an extremely controlling style at work and at home. Any gaps in my self-esteem were covered over with a shell of supreme confidence. Once I had determined a course of action and demonstrated my unwavering confidence in it and in the absence of a clear alternative, others gladly followed.

It should be said that I was in my mid- to late-thirties during my tenure with AUTRON. I had not embarked on any path of personal growth and development. All of my learnings were in the areas of adding management and business skills and competencies. It wasn't until much later that I recognized that a person's way of *being* has a far greater impact than a list of degrees and designations. This may be the single biggest challenge of our time. For the leader to stand up and risk unpopularity and do and say what should be done and said is sadly lacking. This idea is well described in the book by the late Edwin Friedman—*A Failure of Nerve: Leadership in the Age of the Quick Fix.*

My DiSC profile at the time had much more dominance than influence. I only had one way of *being,* and that resulted in an autocratic style of leadership. Growth comes from engaging hearts and minds in a kind of optimism about a possible future. And that requires a very different kind of leadership.

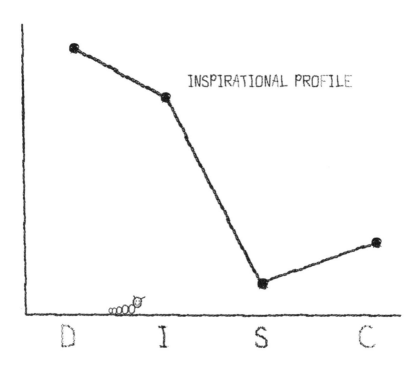

**Figure 5: Author's Former DiSC Behavioral Profile**

After turning forty, I duly entered my midlife meltdown. A completely unnecessary divorce provoked me to resort to a way of handling extreme emotion learned in my youth—I ran away. After a succession of failed relationships, I embarked on a journey of self-discovery. In that process I became convinced—healthily—that I was 100 percent responsible, and I developed some ability to shift my way of *being*. I practiced this skill constantly so that by the time I joined LOFTON, the high-growth real estate company, I was able to successfully operate in a somewhat more flexible and participative leadership style. I cannot pretend that the shift was huge or that I was not and am not still controlling. But my DiSC style shifted measurably.

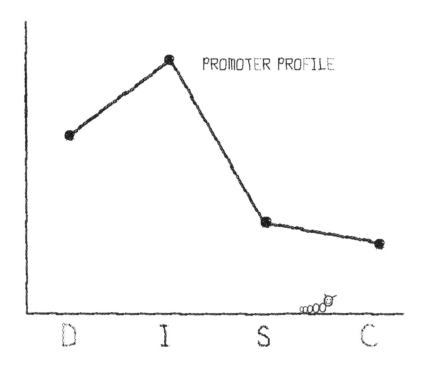

PROMOTER PROFILE

D     I     S     C

**Figure 6: Author's Recent DiSC Behavioral Profile**

There are those who still believe that leaders are born and not made. What I can say from personal experience is that it is possible to develop flexibility in leadership style. It takes time and work, but it can be done. It is achieved in exactly the same way as any behavioral change. The link that I have found most compelling is that just as a leader can go through these changes, so too can corporations. In the case of an individual, it is your own way of *being* that must shift. For an enterprise, it is the culture. Both show up in a DiSC behavioral profile.

### The Need to Shift

Once the turning point has been reached and you are functional, either as an individual or as a company, your way of *be*ing must shift. The downside for an enterprise that does not make this shift is that operating in the survival mode that was once so necessary now becomes progressively more damaging. The easiest way to see this is to consider the risk tolerance of the business. In turnaround, the tolerance is extremely low. A small mistake and the business could fail altogether. But once beyond that point, a company that is not taking at least measured risks is unlikely to grow.

A less obvious effect is that a corporation with a prevalence of an autocratic leadership style is tolerated during tough times, but the best employees start to bail when things improve. Turnover is usually the first sign that an autocratic style will not be tolerated during periods of growth. I have often heard autocratic leaders ask why their best and brightest are leaving just when things are getting better. They fail to understand that the best and brightest demand a voice. They need to feel they are contributing to the firm they loan their skills to.

Such a shift in a way of *be*ing is very hard for an incumbent leader of a failing enterprise. This is why it is often the case in corporate turnarounds that the leader of the enterprise is removed altogether. There is seldom time to wait for a shift. Though it is risky, it is an essential step in the process of turnaround.

During a business turnaround, we certainly should consider whether the leader should stay or leave, but we also need to review all of the stakeholders. There is no practical way to simply fire everyone, so tough choices must be made. Even the "slash and burn" turnaround specialists will take time to review and discover who stands in the way of the turnaround and who supports the effort. It may be that a new bank is needed. Perhaps one or two of the owners are negatively affecting decision making. There will certainly be employees who will thwart needed changes. More often than not there will be customers that must be replaced. Instead of supporting the turnaround, they have typically been a factor in the crisis. Perhaps they have special arrangements that make them much less profitable than other customers.

The customers and suppliers that require the most attention and negatively affect margins are often the ones that an enterprise has become most dependent upon. During a turnaround when a company is in crisis, it is easier to be objective and decide who should go. I have used customer-relationship management (CRM) tools to help build information to make these decisions easier. However, it is also often the case that every customer must be retained, at least in the near term. In these cases, it is vital to set boundaries and start the process to replace them as quickly as possible.

The same is true of employees. In the same way as with existing customers, unless the business is simply massively bloated, it is best in my experience to take a little time. However, it is well known that no leader ever thought that he should have waited a little longer when forced to downsize. The challenge is to discern the difference between those employees who take longer to handle change and those who say they are in favor of planned changes but are passively aggressively resisting. It is the employees who are resisting necessary changes who must be ultimately fired for the turnaround to be successful.

It is probably even more important to "fire" people closest to you when embarking on a personal turnaround. The idea shocks most people, but it is true. I have at several different times in my life ended friendships when so-called friends had already decided who I was and were not supportive of me making changes. Often, friends and relatives will subconsciously influence you to revert to former behavior patterns so you "fit" into their expectations.

This is the point in such a dialog when most people turn to me and ask, "How can I fire my mother/father/brother . . . ?" Moving away is the alternate approach that works for many folks undertaking personal transformation, particularly when there is addictive behavior and it is a case of survival.

For instance, I once knew an individual I'll call Kaitlin who had moved and settled a few hundred miles away from her very dysfunctional family home. Kaitlin maintained almost daily contact with her mother. During every single phone call with her mother, Kaitlin would end up arguing with her about something (trivial) and be upset for some time afterward. She was stuck.

Only a complete break and no contact will provide any chance of recovery when in survival mode. The only way that Kaitlin could ever hope to grow and develop sufficiently to handle her dysfunctional family was to at least initially break free from them. But what happens after the turning point is reached? This is the point during individual transformation when most people surround themselves again with the same dysfunctional people and all the bad habits quickly return. We begin to replay old patterns. New boundaries must be established.

It is very common for individuals with addictions, or at least dysfunctional behavior patterns, to be inexperienced at establishing healthy boundaries. In such cases, unable to provide sufficient self-love and comfort and being so desperate to be loved by others, their needy behavior leads to a failure to set and maintain boundaries to protect them.

While I was dealing with my own challenges, I worked my way through many different books. There are three that are worthy of special mention. The first introduced me to the idea of boundaries. Boundaries are just as important for an enterprise as they are for an individual. One of the most prolific writers on boundaries, Dr. Henry Cloud, published in 2010 *Necessary Endings: The Employees, Businesses, and Relationships That All of Us Have to Give Up in Order to Move Forward*. It seems to me from the title alone that this is an issue that applies as much to businesses as it does to personal transformation.

Both people and entire organizations resist having different boundaries set. In my experience, it takes a series of difficult conversations to establish such boundaries. The conversations that establish these new and healthier boundaries might appropriately be labeled crucial. There are a series of very excellent resources on this subject by Kerry Patterson and others. The second book in this area I want to bring to your attention is called *Crucial Conversations: Tools for Talking When Stakes Are High* (Patterson et al. 2011). The book details how to have tough conversations when the stakes are high and there is much emotion attached. Exactly the situation when boundaries are being redefined.

The third book that provides excellent resources for establishing the bare necessities is Jack Canfield's 2005 book *The Success Principles*. Several of Jack Canfield's success principles are well suited to help support getting the bare necessities in place when in crisis. Principle #25, "Drop out of the 'Ain't it awful club' and surround yourself with successful people" specifically focuses on the idea that you become like the people you spend the most time with. It stresses the importance of avoiding toxic people.

It is not enough to simply fire those toxic people to free you to get through your recovery and reach your own or your enterprise's turning point. Canfield's success principle #29 is "Complete the past to embrace the future." It gives a series of tools that can be used to forgive. Forgiveness is the only way to relieve you of the emotional burden attached to these relationships. Otherwise moving away or even firing such toxic people will not be enough to free you to recover.

One more success principle that is particularly helpful in the survival mode is success principle #44: "Find a wing to climb under." As the name suggests, it stresses the importance of talking to those who have successfully chartered the turbulent waters you are experiencing. We tend to ask our friends, relatives, or a consultant about things that they have never experienced themselves.

If we have been clear to define what constitutes recovery for us and stayed focused on getting functional; if we have summoned the willpower to make necessary changes and established a support network, a wing to climb under, to hold us accountable in our quest; if we have taken real action to not simply stop that which was harming us but replace it with nonaddictive, functional habits; then and only then can we embark on a journey that will get us to where we want to go. We must next decide our future. Once we are functional, we must shift to growth and development. We *can* grow and develop toward a future that is waiting for us. We *can* grow and develop to implement our true purpose.

Chapter Four

# On Purpose: A Sense of Meaning
# Makes Everything Easier

It was an Aha! moment. Virginia Woolf called such
little epiphanies "moments of being," when a shock
pulls the gauzy curtain off everyday existence and
throws a sudden floodlight on what our lives are
really about. There is another side to this mountain. It
was time to go into training for the journey. But now
I felt an inward trust. I could be creative again.

—Gail Sheehy, *Passages:*
*Predictable Crises of Adult Life*

If you have read the preceding chapters, then you will
have realized that so far in our journey our growth and
development have been a continuing struggle. It has taken
conscious effort and energy to develop and sustain awareness
sufficient to get real about our situation. But finally we have
grown enough to understand and appreciate where we are.
Having achieved that level, we probably discovered that we
needed to get our company, or indeed ourselves, functional
in some ways. Now, at least, we are beyond mere survival.
But once we have met these bare necessities, whether as
an individual or as part of a company, we typically begin to
question why. We ask, "What is the point of it all?"

It is identifying some purpose that relieves the continuing struggle. Instead of operating from a place of fear there is a point to everything. The sense of meaning makes the journey easier. More meaningful. More purposeful. More.

Many of us reach the middle of our hectic lives and question the point of everything. I was no different. The midlife passage is well documented. Everything is effectively thrown in the air and reconsidered. Is this all there is? Should I be doing something else? Am I really happy? Is this the best I can do? Is it too late for something new? For many the exercise is an unsettling period of a year or two and then everything kind of drops back into place. For others it provokes a massive change in lifestyle and living. For a lucky few, it leads to the discovery of more meaning for their lives than they previously experienced. They find a purpose that seems to help everything in their lives make sense, perhaps for the first time.

By the way, according to the book *Passages: Predictable Crises of Adult Life,* this process occurs every eight to twelve years for every individual (Sheehy 1974). This aligns well to the idea about enterprises going through stages of growth too. It must be said though that things have changed in the past twenty years. Gail Sheehy's newer book from 1995, *New Passages: Mapping Your Life across Time,* makes a compelling case for a much more conscious shift to a new stage of life. This book advocates that your enterprise also make that very conscious shift—to one inspired by purpose.

By way of example, imagine an enterprise that has found a comfortable situation. It has a good share of what seems a pretty stable market and makes acceptable margins without too much special effort. Often it lives in denial of the changes going on around the company. Driven predominantly by fear of losing what it already "has," the company is stuck and afraid of trying anything new. But there is a problem. If a business is not growing and developing, then it is decaying. It is dying a slow death. I appreciate that this sounds a little extreme, but there is no stasis. Everything around us is changing, and we must change too in order to even survive. The good news is that newfound energy is discovered when we assign a purpose to what we are doing. The ongoing struggle of mere survival gives way to something that feels much easier. More natural. Purposeful.

## *The Ultimate Purpose*

There is something very special that happens when either an individual or a company shifts to a life with purpose. Most people at least once in their lives have been involved with a team united to achieve a very definite purpose. The team's purpose evokes passion in everyone on the team and anyone associated with the team. Everything seems to happen more easily. There is boundless energy, and every separate task seems somehow connected to the team's purpose. Can you remember being a member of such a team?

The same boundless energy experienced by a team with a shared purpose comes from alignment between different ways of being—physical, psychological, intellectual, emotional, and spiritual. For example, some individuals develop their physical selves to an advanced level. But in other areas of their lives, perhaps their behavior in relationships, they keep repeating the same mistakes. Or maybe an individual invests great effort in thinking through different aspects of his or her life and so is intellectually well developed but at the same time is perhaps emotionally very immature. It is alignment that alleviates the struggles that seem to plague everything that we do. But how do we identify the purpose around which we can align and so get past this perennial struggle we experience?

There is a wonderful book called *The Rhythm of Life* that introduces our true purpose as becoming the best version of ourselves (Kelly 1999). That is, the "point" of it all is for an individual to grow and develop. Could it be the same for a company? Well, the process of evolution by natural selection is said to involve three things: (1) More individuals are produced than can possibly survive, (2) traits vary considerably between individuals, and (3) certain traits are passed from one generation to another.

It *is* helpful to think about a whole organization as evolving in the same way as humans evolve. That is, more companies are formed than will survive; traits vary considerably between companies; and certain lessons are captured and "passed" from one company to another. Maybe, then, the point of any company is to evolve. Its purpose in effect is to become the best version of itself. It certainly does not hurt to think of an enterprise this way.

### How Will You Be?

If the point of the journey is to evolve, then the mission, vision, values, and goals for an individual or for an enterprise are the means and mechanism by which we get from where we are to where we want to be. This chapter covers the mission, vision, and values. A mission is the reason for doing something and may be a sentence or two. A vision is a description of some end point. Typically a vision is a few inspiring sentences that outline a possible future. Values are the things that are important to us along the way, such as competence or contribution. They are usually a list of perhaps eight characteristics. It is essential to generate a mission and a vision to develop clarity about where we are headed. Without somewhere in mind, how will we know we have arrived? Values provide a kind of guideline for how we live our lives. One way to appreciate values is to see them as preferred characteristics that will guide the style we will demonstrate to get where we are going.

Some individuals and some corporations, such as Amazon.com, develop separate missions, visions, and lists of values: "Our vision is to be earth's most customer-centric company; to build a place where people can come to find and discover anything they might want to buy online."

Other corporations, like Starbucks, blend their mission, vision, and value statements:

Establish Starbucks as the premier purveyor of the finest coffee in the world while maintaining our uncompromising principles as we grow. The following six guiding principles will help us measure the appropriateness of our decisions:

- Provide a great work environment and treat each other with respect and dignity.
- Embrace diversity as an essential component in the way we do business.
- Apply the highest standards of excellence to the purchasing, roasting, and fresh delivery of our coffee.
- Develop enthusiastically satisfied customers all of the time.
- Contribute positively to our communities and our environment.
- Recognize that profitability is essential to our future success.

Having first established that our purpose is to evolve, we typically move to develop our vision, then our mission, and finally our values. Here is where it gets tricky.

**I am going to suggest that we do something *completely* different.**

We have all been taught to start with the end in mind. How else can we know where we are headed? We have learned that we should first develop what we want to have in our vision. We commit to how we will accomplish our vision by next defining our mission. Our mission guides us in what we will do to achieve our vision. The poster on the wall of the boardroom invariably first describes our vision and then our mission and ends with our guidelines for how we will be in the form of a set of corporate values. I am going to suggest that we do not start with the end in mind. We shall leave our vision, which is what we want to *have*, until last. I am also going to suggest that we delay thinking about what we will do to achieve our vision. We shall leave our mission, which is what we must *do*, until later. I want to start instead with who we are. I want to begin with our values; that is, how we will *be*.

In chapter 1 the idea was introduced of *being* responsible. By *being* responsible we will have more things that we can *do* to ensure that we *have* the results we seek. Most of us have been raised to believe that we need to *have* things in our lives so that we can *do* what we want and so we can then *be* who it is we want to be. For example, when I *have* more time I will *do* more things with my children so I can *be* a better parent. The equivalent for our enterprise might be when we *have* a better product we can *do* more sales and *be* a leader in our market.

One of the basic tenets of the world of self-improvement is the reversal of the *have-do-be* principle. In the language of self-improvement, "havingness" does not produce "beingness," but the other way around. The idea is that *being* the person you want to be allows you to *do* the things such a person would do so you can *have* what it is you want. Most individuals might say that they want to *have* financial independence. They might believe that they will not *be* happy until they *have* their financial independence. Worse, many take no action and *do* little to achieve their financial independence.

A basic example of this occurred at SIPTON. Recall that SIPTON is a long-established and family-owned and run commercial real estate firm. The company held on to an almost oppressive dress code for the longest time. They believed that they had to tell people what to *do* (how to dress). Instead they could have declared how they wanted their company to *be* (professional). They had fallen into the trap of valuing how to dress (doingness) rather than maintaining professionalism (beingness).

So instead of worrying about what we want to *have* (our vision) or even how we will achieve our vision by deciding what we must *do* (our mission), what we focus on instead is first how we will *be* (our values). What we value will define how we are going to *be*.

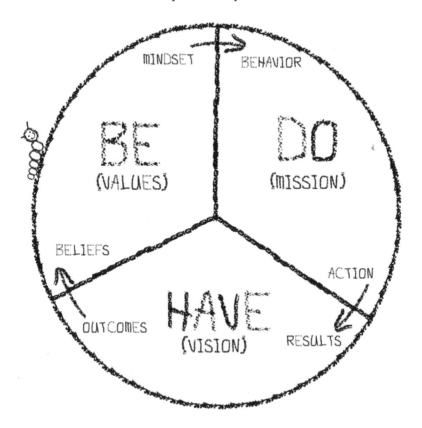

**Figure 7: Be-Do-Have**

But how is it that we can consciously shift our values? How can we change our ways of *being*? Well, the way to *be* a certain way is to make a choice in each moment to actually perform the action of *do*ing something in line with that way of *being*. Are you *being* the person or the company you said you were going to *be*? Perhaps you decide that your organization will *be* confident, for example. Imagine that you have been able to encourage everyone in the enterprise to think and move through their corporate lives as members of a confident organization. The actions more and more employees are *do*ing are based on what everyone thinks about *being* confident. Do more and more employees believe that the company is confident? Can they see themselves behaving this way? Do they feel good when individuals and teams are *do*ing confident things? The enterprise practices and practices *be*ing confident. With repeated practice, the members of the company will learn what it means to *be* confident. By *being* confident and *do*ing confident things, the business starts to *have* improved results. Customers and competitors start to make comments and observations. The business continues to move in this way until it eventually becomes an unconscious way of *be*ing. It becomes a new habit.

Did I mention that this was tricky?

One way to think about how to *be* a certain something is to consider it as a state of mind. Perhaps we want to *be* creative, courageous, or maybe confident as in the last corporate example. The new state of mind is clearly going to be affected by our values, beliefs, and our attitudes—our mind-set. And this framework is then further affected by how we feel in the moment—our emotional state. When combined, all of these things directly affect your behavior—what you *do*. What we are essentially trying to accomplish is to shift our entire state of mind. This can be achieved for an entire corporate culture too.

Let us see again how this works in real organizations. Recall that AUTRON was a start-up defined by its only product. As soon as the business had achieved turnaround, the company was left with engineering talent to sell and no product. Instead it focused on a single value—*being* reliable. Through frequent practice, the organization shifted to a reliable way of *being*. It found many ways to demonstrate *being* reliable, from following up on all inquiries the same day to completing major projects on time and within budget.

WIZARD, the cable test equipment provider, set out to *be* dominant in its chosen market and *be* the leader. It quickly developed sophisticated marketing to accurately identify customer needs. The voice of the customer in turn forced the company to address its design and manufacturing challenges. It quickly built world-class product-development and manufacturing capabilities to match its marketing prowess. What is of particular note is that the general manager himself was a particularly strong leader with a background steeped in marketing. As is so often the case, the particular focus and strength of the leader tends to influence much of the company's way of *being*. A very financially oriented leader can often unconsciously result in the company *being* more financially focused. A very sales-oriented leader can often cause the company to *be* more sales focused.

By way of another example, AUBURN, the communications test equipment company, embarked on an entirely different way of *being* after a series of mergers and acquisitions. To bring about a complete shift in the way all its stakeholders were *being*, AUBURN more and more narrowly defined itself as a global leader in something until it became true. Everyone in the enterprise was trained. Everyone learned what it meant to *be* a global leader. As more and more members of the enterprise were convinced how to *be* a global leader, actions followed. By taking action, by *doing* those things that a global leader would *do*, the company was on the path to *have* the results of a global leader.

But all of this is easier said than done.

Recent brain theory research has confirmed that it takes considerable effort to shift our way of *being*. In actual fact it consumes extra glucose to effect any change of mind. Any attempt to modulate our behavior, for example, takes measurable conscious effort. In his 2011 book *Thinking, Fast and Slow*, Daniel Kahneman said, "When you are actively involved in difficult cognitive reasoning or engaged in a task that requires self-control, your blood glucose level drops" (43). The book does an excellent job of explaining the different roles and functions of the conscious and unconscious parts of our thinking. Is it any different in our organizations to shift an established and largely unconscious way of *being*? Perhaps it is not surprising that we have all experienced the additional effort involved in overcoming our unconscious ways of *being* and driving any kind of sea change in an enterprise.

If it takes that much energy to make such a shift, why would values, or *being*, come first? Well, *being* is a kind of shortcut to *do* things in a different way. If someone tried to teach you all the myriad ways of *do*ing things to display confidence, it would take a very long time. Instead, if you have observed someone *being* confident you already have a sense of what that is like. You are more readily able to figure out for yourself what to *do* to display confidence. You essentially cannot *do* confidence; only *be* confident and then *do* things that display your confidence. You must first shift your way of *being*. Make sense?

Let us be clear though that if the organization is going out of business and already devoted to falling from the airplane without a parachute, as it were, then it is not functional. No amount of effort will achieve a shift in ways of *being*. This approach cannot work. The work described in earlier chapters of this book must first be completed as much for an individual as for an organization. In summary, abandon victimhood and enter a state of awareness, develop rituals to stay aware, use a process of inquiry to get real, and then get functional so you have the resources to move beyond mere existence. Then, and only then, can you work to shift your ways of *being*.

There is a potential problem in shifting your ways of *being*. Some believe that you should "fake it until you make it" to effect a change in ways of *being*. The idea is that you "act as if." The thinking is that the person or the organization that you were *being* in the past is not going to individually or collectively think, act, or react in a way that will achieve the new desired result, so you must *pretend*. But it is *not possible* to fool even yourself let alone an entire enterprise. It must be believable. There must be hope. If there is insincerity, a shift in ways of *being* will again simply not work. So how can we genuinely shift our ways of *being*?

The right way to accomplish a shift in ways of *being* is best shown with an example. If we want to *be* fearless ourselves, we must first cause others to be fearless. This must be done sincerely and not for personal gain. Perhaps we take an unusual risk and agree to pay for a service or product in advance to encourage another organization or an individual to overcome their fear of failure and take a risk. The very act of giving something away like this—to promote fearlessness in another—yields a most interesting result. You cannot give something away that you do not have yourself. You are forced to develop a new thought. That thought is that you must yourself be fearless. Otherwise how could you be giving fearlessness away? As Mahatma Gandhi said, "*Be* the change that you wish to see in the world" (emphasis mine). You can appreciate that you cannot give away something you do not have.

Interestingly, creating a way of *being* in others so that you can develop it in yourself works every bit as well for an enterprise as it does for an individual. An individual might dwell upon the list of values and select their list of ways of *being*. The exercise is a little different for a corporation. To promote buy-in and create enough inertia for the selected values to become established requires involving and engaging as many employees in the process as possible.

## *Your Brand*

There is a direct link between this focus on ways of *being* and branding. Just as products have a brand identity, whole corporations and, yes, even individuals can have a brand. There has been a great deal written about personal branding since it was first presented by Tom Peters over ten years ago.

One of the most well-known names to explore this topic is Dan Schawbel, who is, according to *Forbes* magazine, widely considered the go-to expert on personal branding. The most important message in Dan's 2010 book *Me 2.0: 4 Steps to Building Your Future* is that in order to be successful in the new world of work, you have to be the commander of your career (431). He said, "We cannot rely on our teachers, parents, managers and friends to make us successful. Instead we have to take ownership of our careers and put our passions in motion, in order to achieve our dreams. To be a commander means to be authentic, transparent, confident, persistent, and display leadership." *Do you not think it interesting that these are all ways of* be*ing?* "A commander is a state-of-mind and in order to help you unlock the commander inside of you, I wrote this book to navigate you through my personal branding process." It is even more interesting that he should reference a state of mind, don't you think? Dan begins by suggesting that we each discover our own personal brand.

Whether we take an active role in our own brand or simply let it "happen," we surely all have a personal brand. Our own personal brand is the perception by others of how we are *being.* But we have an opportunity to shape our own personal brand and to build equity in that brand. Before we can proactively build our own brand equity we must first discover our own personal brand. In the past, this has been taken to mean that we should attach some artificial associations to our product and so encourage more people to buy it. Corporate and personal brands today are rather different.

With the incredible transparency of the social networks, it has become more and more essential to be authentic in the way that we present ourselves. It is now typical for recruiters to first explore the social media when considering a candidate for a role. No longer is it even possible to ignore the social media. Everyone must be cognizant of what others might be saying about you. Your brand is out there whether you take ownership for it or not. The same is true for companies. Walmart's use of Facebook back in 2007 to support their back-to-school campaign backfired for exactly this reason. They claimed a brand character of *style* that was inauthentic. We are moving increasingly toward more and more transparency in our dealings and a more authentic presentation of our enterprises. It is this alignment between our real selves as individuals or businesses and those we serve that eliminates the "struggle."

| | | | |
|---|---|---|---|
| able | eager | known | self-reliant |
| accountable | energetic | maverick | serious |
| altruistic | fearless | opportunistic | straightforward |
| assertive | flexible | organized | success oriented |
| authentic | focused | passionate | tenacious |
| bold | great | powerful | thriving |
| collaborative | hardworking | professional | unstoppable |
| compassionate | honorable | proud | versatile |
| confident | imaginative | reliable | well prepared |
| courageous | inspirational | resourceful | wise |
| dependable | intentional | results oriented | |

**Figure 8: Example Ways of Being**

My own personal brand promise is to make a difference by *be*ing positively inspiring, healthy, abundant, wise, connected, committed, courageous, learning, growing, and loving. Somewhere in the list of values in the figure above are six or maybe ten different values that will have a much greater meaning to you. But the brand-promise discovery exercise can be difficult for an entire enterprise, especially a large one.

In order to help employees identify how they perceived themselves at the time, and again in the future, SIPTON asked them to identify the company as a type of car. The majority saw themselves as a '57 Chevy, though most aspired to *be* a modern American-built Ford. By using this analogy it became much easier to identify a believable corporate brand.

Again, most of us will be worried that the values we have selected are not "right." Understand that in the same way a mission and vision will develop over time, so too will your values. Once you have practiced a way of *be*ing, you will eventually become unconsciously competent. You may eventually no longer need to constantly remind yourself to practice *be*ing, say, confident. It has, with practice, become part of who you are. It is no different for a company.

### Mission and Vision

With how we want to *be* firmly captured in our list of values, we turn now to our mission and vision. We are looking to define where it is we want to be and what we will do to get there.

The human mind is a goal-seeking machine. Whether consciously or unconsciously, we set goals, and our brains look for resources to get us from where we are to where we want to be. We establish something called cognitive dissonance. It provides a motivational drive to close the gaps between thoughts, beliefs, values, and emotions. We are driven to close the gap between how things are and how we want them to be. When magnets of opposing polarity are brought close together they attract one another. The closer they are to one another the stronger the pull. When they are almost touching, the strength of the draw between them is at its strongest. When the gap is small between how things are and how we want them to be, or cognitive dissonance is at its least, the energy to close the gap is strongest.

One problem frequently experienced is that unless the mission and vision is believable we will not generate cognitive dissonance. We will simply ignore it. If the mission and vision is believable and is something to which we can relate, we develop hope. With hope comes the energy to move from where we are to where we want to be. One of my clients once insisted on a vision so grandiose as to be laughable. It was so unbelievable that there was never any hope of it being achieved. Employees worked diligently and very creatively to undermine the vision. Over a two-year period it completely disappeared.

Another common problem is where a company has a mission and vision that fail to generate any passion. A select few executives return from a retreat at some exotic venue and present the output of their work to groans and sighs from employees. Instead of bonding workers around a common purpose, it alienates them even more. The mission and vision become required boxes to check and are repeatedly rolled out in marketing messaging. The mission and vision are so far removed from how the company is really *being* that even stakeholders pay no attention to the mission and vision.

It is not the mission and vision as a product that is important here. It is the process of developing the mission and vision to get clear about where we are headed that is key. Apple is a company that plays at the edge of art and technology to meet needs we do not know we have yet. They see a future where everyone and everything is connected. In contrast to their published "mission statement," their *real* mission and their vision are implanted deeply in the culture of Apple.

So how is it that we can embed a mission and vision into the culture of our company? The answer is not to inflict one on the company but to let it manifest on its own. It is already there buried deep in the shared experiences and future possibilities of the enterprise. It is not outside somewhere. It is already within. Of course, there is a danger that the loudest individuals or those in positions of power and influence will act to protect or preserve their status and artificially limit future possibilities. A process that truly gives the quiet and thoughtful members the same voice as those in leadership roles is paramount.

But how is it that we know we chose the right mission and the best aspirational yet still achievable vision? Like the values, the point is that there is no single right answer. The process will need to be repeated when the environment changes or as the organization grows and develops anyway. Contrary to popular belief, it is not a once-every-ten-years process. It is a tool to support growth and development. Not the other way around.

Many individuals and many companies operate with a belief that they have not found what they are looking for and life or business will become easy once they discover what it is they *should* be doing. There is a fear that they may have taken a wrong turn and that is why everything appears to be such a huge struggle.

Whether or not you subscribe to the view that everything happens for a reason, it is true that everything that has happened in the past shapes who you are today. In the same way, the history of an enterprise helps make it what it is today. The future is based on the choices that we make today. Now. So our future is full of the possibilities we can recognize now. Problem—what we see as possibilities is entirely distorted by who we have become. Our past conspires to limit the choices we have in our future. That is, if we remain unconscious.

If we are being real about our situation—that is, if we can stay conscious enough for long enough—then we will see unlimited possibilities. At once, you realize that you are the product of everything that has happened to you and that your future possibilities are boundless. Jack Canfield is fond of saying that courage is not the absence of fear. The secret is to feel the fear and do whatever it was you were afraid of doing anyway. Limitless possibilities appear when you are conscious and courageous.

So how is it that we can consciously consider limitless possibilities yet identify a believable mission and vision that evokes passion? The starting point is to reflect on our natural talents and developed skills. The work on positive psychology by Martin E. P. Seligman, PhD, in his 2002 book *Authentic Happiness* stresses that real happiness comes from playing to your strengths. Your strengths are a combination of natural talents and learned skills. In the same way, a company that experiences less "struggle" is one that sticks to the knitting and plays to its strengths. The key to a successful mission and vision is one that stretches the individual or the company but inspires the actions needed by playing to your strengths and creating a manageable gap between where you are and where you want to be.

Playing to your strengths is akin to doing what comes naturally or "following your bliss" as Joseph Campbell is quoted in the 2004 book, *Pathways to Bliss*. Importantly, in his work Campbell says we must guide ourselves either by the example of another or by following our own bliss. Campbell defines bliss as a deep sense of being present, of doing what you absolutely must do to be yourself.

Even so, putting a focus on what comes naturally and using that to discover a mission and a vision that inspires is difficult. I worked with Jack Canfield for several years to become one of his very first personal-transformation trainers. Part of that work entailed discovering my own purpose. I found it to be the single most difficult exercise I had ever undertaken. It took me two years of work to discover my own bliss: to use my insight and my passion to inspire others to grow. It was not until I developed an entire training class on developing your personal brand that I was reminded of a little timeless wisdom. You attempt to teach others what you (yourself) most need to learn. It is said that we really cannot know something until we have taught others.

If your bliss is difficult to find, Campbell provides an alternative approach. We can use the example of another to guide us in our quest. Again, this is as true for an individual as it is for a company. Business literature is full of examples of employees leaving the confines of a large organization that is no longer listening to establish a new competitor. There are even more examples of trade delegations traveling the world and visiting very disparate companies. They return with new insight and even clearer pictures of themselves—who they are and what they can be. If you or your companies are unsure of your bliss, travel. Modeling others is the absolute best way to discover who you are and to learn where it is you want to go and what to do to get there.

Everything is now centered on a sense of purpose. We have now established our purpose as *being* the very best that we can be. We have identified the values that we hold dear. Some are based on our strengths, while others we aspire to. They will require achievable growth and development. We work to create these ways of *being* in others so we may learn that we have them to give away. We get clear about where we are headed and how we will get there. Our mission and vision is believable and evokes passion. And we realize that it will grow and develop as the individual or the organization grows and develops. So how do we achieve our vision? Goals inside a vision turn visionary dreams to reality, energizing everything you do with meaning, enthusiasm, and fun. With your ways of *being* aligned with a purposeful direction, achieving your goals is less of a struggle. Let's see how.

Chapter Five

# A Chunk at a Time:
# Achieving Uncommon Results

Goals. There's no telling what you can do when you
get inspired by them. There's no telling what you can
do when you believe in them. There's no telling what
will happen when you act upon them.
—Jim Rohn

Now we have our values, our mission, and our vision. If we
have followed the steps laid out in this book, then we know
where we are and where we want to be. We know what we will
do in order to have what we want. We have developed a dream
of what could be. And we are functional enough to have the
resources to get where we want to go. Our next step is to get it
done. But how?

The answer is to set goals. In this instance, it is much more
common for companies to have some system for setting
goals than individuals do. More established businesses have
very sophisticated systems for establishing goals. But what
is somewhat surprising is the shortage of goal setting on an
individual level. Why is that? Perhaps for many of us, our
parents never modeled the setting of goals. Perhaps we tried
to set some personal goals, only to be discouraged and even
teased by our friends and colleagues for setting them. We
declare, "I'll get fit by going to the gym four times a week" or
"I'll lose fifteen pounds," but then we have trouble following

through on our intentions. We may simply have a built-in fear of failure or rejection that acts as a limiting belief and stops us from even attempting to set goals for ourselves. However, without specific goals our actions cannot be coordinated in a way to help us live our mission and reach our vision. Without *do*ing the things we must do to *be* the person or the company we want to be, we cannot *have* our vision. In chapter 3 we stressed the need to take action. Being in perfect alignment with what it is you want *is* important but does not obviate the need to take action. The goals are the essential doingness of life.

When people have goals to guide them, they are happier and achieve more than they would without having them. It is a brain thing. Achieving a goal you have set produces dopamine, a neurotransmitter responsible for feelings of pleasure. Reciprocally, dopamine activates neural circuitry that makes you eager to pursue new challenges. Goals also provide focus. Goals provide a measuring stick for progress. Goals enhance productivity. They bolster self-esteem. And most of all, goals increase commitment, so you're more likely to achieve whatever you set out to conquer.

One of the principles taught in the world of personal transformation is to take your dreams and divide (chunk) them down into more manageable, bite-sized goals. I have worked with many leadership teams that freeze at this point. They simply do not know how to get from where they are to where they want to be, either for themselves or their organizations. They tend to adopt goals that they believe will move them incrementally forward instead of goals that move them toward where they really want to be. They are caught in the trap of fine-tuning efficiency and leave their effectiveness to chance. Again, the world of personal development has something to teach us. There are two key elements. The first is to model others. In the world today, it has never been easier to learn from the experiences of others. Someone has done either all or part of what you want to do or perhaps even failed at the attempt. Either way, there are things that can be learned from the experience. Most great start-ups were born of disenchanted employees leaving a larger company that could no longer hear them. Learning from others is something we do very naturally.

It should be stressed that it is important to learn from others rather than simply copy. Leaders who were unable to complete a project at a former company can often be caught trying to repeat exactly the same project to prove it was not they that failed. This is a dangerous trap. Instead, study the successful and unsuccessful behaviors of others to learn lessons for your own or your company's journey.

The second element has to do with getting even clearer about where it is you want to go. In the world of personal development, a great deal more emphasis is placed on imagining what it will be like—this place we want to go. I am not advocating daily meditation for your entire enterprise, though it might be interesting to explore how it could be adapted. However, it is very common for the values, mission, and vision to simply be "announced" with PowerPoint slides. The essence of leadership is to enroll others in a shared vision. There is no shortcut to the many conversations that lead to a shared alignment around where it is you want the company to go.

At AUTRON, the British software company I was brought in to help turn around, the mission and vision were openly discussed. Everyone in the business was made acutely aware that it was all about cash-generating growth. It was the constant conversation not only inside the company but with customers too. In fact, there never were any PowerPoint presentations about where the company wanted to go—only conversations.

Modeling others and getting clear about where it is you want to go now make it possible to chunk the big picture down into a series of goals. By using mind-mapping or basic project-management tools, the vision is progressively broken down into smaller and smaller pieces. But there is danger lurking here. It is easier to invest time analyzing, planning, and organizing than it is to take action. Successful people and successful companies are action oriented.

For commercial real estate developer LOFTON, to achieve its ambitious growth plans entailed getting very clear about where the company was headed. Modeling other commercial real estate firms that had grown aggressively brought up an otherwise hidden problem. Relying on a single product group (such as retail, industrial, healthcare, or office) exposes the business to even more extreme cyclic effects than the usual seven-to-ten-year cycle. LOFTON elected to expand to all four of the listed product groups to help smooth out the cycles. The rest of the growth came from geographic expansion by adding regional offices.

By researching what other companies had done and where they had opened regional offices, the risk of failure was substantially reduced. Progressively, more goals were developed to help get the organization where it wanted to go. Many subsequent conversations led to hundreds of related goals to achieve the company's more than 1,000 percent growth in less than three years. It is important to note that many of the initial goals were refined or even abandoned as the company collected more feedback about what was moving them closer to their vision and what was moving them away.

SIPTON, another real estate developer, chunked down where it wanted to go using an annual goal-setting process with three levels. Each year there would be a different corporate "theme" with a single goal shared by everyone in the enterprise. For example, one year the goal to "develop accountability" was established. The second tier of goals was department- or workgroup-specific. Finally, the third tier of goals was specific to each individual employee.

Many companies and individuals clearly know and accept the value of goal setting but get stuck in the mode of simply going through the motions year after year. Recall that the way you do anything is the way you do everything. If the prevailing culture of your organization is to be very detail- and plan-oriented, then there will be a great reluctance to take bold action without first having all the i's dotted and t's crossed. Unless you are prepared to take a risk, you will likely opt for safety and simply check the box. Such goals are doubtless useful in bringing incremental improvements but will not get you where you really want to go. The point of leaning into it and being willing to pay the price is that no amount of planning can guarantee an outcome. It is the feedback you will get on the way that will help you correct your actions to move you closer to where you ultimately want to be. The interesting thing about not waiting until everything is perfect is that you are much more open to learning, knowing that you do not know everything. All the while you are building momentum in the organization. This is exactly what happened at LOFTON.

### *Four More Ways*

There are four more quite neat concepts often used in the personal-development field to help individuals achieve their goals that apply very effectively to the corporate world.

### a) Daily Steps

This approach encourages you to take a certain number of actions toward the completion of your goals every single day—usually five. This tends to work better in action-oriented functions like sales and customer service. It creates a great deal of activity, all of it in support of the goals.

## b) Emotional Goals

A second concept is something that has been referred to as *emotional goals*. These are not the task-oriented goals that we are more used to but instead are related to the dreams we have as youngsters that seem to get discarded, ignored, or at least considered less important than our task-oriented goals. They are centered on security, respect, involvement, freedom, and excitement. They tend to be inextricably linked to our life purpose. There is an equivalent in the corporate world. I worked as a consultant to GGS. The company was founded on general systems technology, from where they took their name. At the time when I worked with them, there were no business goals remotely related to the original vision of the founder. When I asked about the history, the owner came alive. He talked with great excitement and passion about the original purpose of the business.

As a child we might have unhealthy emotional goals, such as seeking attention or obtaining instant gratification. There are both unhealthy and healthy emotional goals in an enterprise too. LOFTON's original and ambitious goal to become a leader in its field was usurped by a less healthy goal to simply grow large.

## c) Enabling Goals

A third and related concept is to focus on enabling goals; that is, goals specifically related to improved habits that will support higher levels of performance. For example, it was decided that adding shared services centrally at LOFTON would help lower operating costs. Hosting services like accounting, property management, marketing, IT, and HR in one location and having twelve regional offices share these services demanded a level of matrix management. Missing were the understanding and the habits to support matrix management. Specific enabling goals had to be developed to help master matrix management involving training, modified organizational structures, job descriptions, and coaching. The result was to add matrix management as a competence that supported not only a shared-service model but also the successful sharing of many other specialist resources, making the business substantially more efficient.

## d) The Breakthrough Goal

Most of our goals to this point have served to improve our individual or our company lives in the moment. The fourth concept in the world of self-development is the breakthrough goal. It is a goal that up-levels every other goal and upgrades everything you do. It is a goal that would be worth pursuing with extra passion. It is usually so big that it would take focus and action every day over a longer period of time. So, in contrast to the idea of chunking our goals down to be manageable, it is a single larger goal that will take consistent and continuous action to achieve.

A personal example is the very book you are reading. Writing a book based on a career is a significant undertaking. It takes action every day over an extended period of time, perhaps because I am from the school of two-finger typing! Yet this is very much a breakthrough goal for me. It permits me to significantly up-level my career in many ways. Without worrying about how or whether you could achieve such a goal, what one single goal could quantum leap you or your business to the next level?

The high-technology company INSOL had a vision to develop the world's most advanced safety-critical control system. Developing such a technology required more resources than the company had at the time. In order to successfully deploy such an advanced system, it would also need access to more markets in more industries to make it viable.

INSOL established a goal to become a public company. A single goal to transform itself into a public company would give the business access to the resources it would need to achieve its vision. Joining the world of public companies would provide access to new and more powerful partnerships. The funds raised would permit it to acquire companies that could use the new technology to serve other industries. INSOL did become a public company, accomplishing its breakthrough goal. Its new status as a public company helped it attract the largest grant ever awarded by the Offshore Supplies Office of the British government to help fund an award-winning product development. It used funds successfully raised in two rounds of funding to acquire a number of companies to build a group that would go on to be the single largest supplier of safety-critical systems to the world.

As with the other goals, it is important to visualize its completion. What would you be doing, seeing, and feeling? It is perhaps even more important to practice visualization of a breakthrough goal because of the need to reinspire yourself or your company to maintain commitment. But there is another effect that is particularly important. In the field of neurolinguistic programming (NLP), there is a technique for rapid rehearsal, which is particularly helpful when implementing breakthrough goals.

## *Rapid Rehearsal*

The rapid-rehearsal technique first involves exploring what you will experience once you have achieved your goal. It is important to see what you will see, hear what you will hear, and feel what you will feel. It is almost as if you could *taste* it. Once the goal is achieved, the idea is to fully experience the sense of what it is like and also what lies beyond the breakthrough goal. What other goals can now be accomplished? How much closer am I to my ultimate vision?

So how does this work? A number of experiential workshops use a particular example to help demonstrate how this works. The facilitator will set up the exercise and have everyone standing with his or her eyes closed. The idea is that you are taken through a process where you imagine that you are moving toward a ledge on a tall building. Many people actually experience the fear associated with being in such a dangerous position. The exercise is then repeated, except this time you are told to imagine that you can fly! The fear dissipates. It serves to demonstrate that your mind does not differentiate between real and imagined experiences. If you can imagine experiencing having achieved your goal, and only if you can stimulate the same emotional experience, then your mind will effectively rehearse the means by which it can achieve the goal.

Having visited the goal and seen the future, it is time to look around and explore the process your mind created to get you there. This essentially involves walking beside the path in your mind that brought you to this point and re-experiencing the journey. Some of it will be clear and fully experienced, and other parts of the path will be less clear to you. As you look at the pathway, you will notice specific steps. These steps will include resources or help you received on the way, specific actions that were taken, and new skills and abilities mastered on the way to the achievement of the breakthrough goal. You may well wonder how on earth you get to experience this journey that in reality you have not yet accomplished. That's the magic. Your unconscious mind does not know the difference. The wonderful goal-setting machine that is your brain is already figuring out ways to get this breakthrough goal completed.

The equivalent in an organization is the planning process. Most project-management methodologies put a great deal of emphasis on the sequence of the steps needed to get something done. Much of the time and focus is on the interdependencies of the tasks needed to accomplish a given goal. What must be done in what sequence to get the work completed? While some planning is required to ensure that essential dependencies are known and understood, planning often becomes an end in itself rather than a means to an end.

Corporate planning should not be about producing plans that will never be read or referred to until the next annual planning session. It is a process. One of the key elements of a successful transformation is using a planning process to enroll. So, what is it to enroll? The field of change management often refers to the need to generate emotional buy-in to your values, mission, and vision or goal. Enrollment is less about having someone say that they agree to a particular course of action and more about being emotionally engaged. Individuals become emotionally engaged when they understand how a particular course of action not only meets a need but also aligns with their own values and beliefs. This alignment can only be discovered through conversation.

It is helpful to structure these conversations around phases of work. Everyone finds it easier to cope with a shorter time frame and some pretty explicit objectives. The alternative is to attempt to guess how the whole process of corporate transformation will go and then attempt to get support and commitment to something that is probably going to take two or three years to accomplish.

In the past, singularly dominant individuals typically led commercial real estate companies. SIPTON was no different. It had built a reputation for win-lose scenarios and was difficult for brokers and tenants alike to work with. As a part of its transformation, a detailed three-year plan to effectively rebrand the entire business failed to develop much, if any, interest. It was simply too much to imagine in a single step. However, a first step of upgrading the look of the company's marketing collateral was readily understood and accepted. It served to move the company toward the rebranding it needed.

### *Plan for the Unexpected*

Having broken down the huge dream into manageable pieces, the next challenge is indeed to figure out where to start. The world of project management would simply have us analyze what must be done before anything else. Each prerequisite is placed in sequence in a PERT chart. A PERT chart simply arranges prerequisite tasks in a structure that can be used to minimize the time to complete the project. The path through the tasks of greatest duration, the critical path, defines the duration of the whole project. The required resources are overlaid to the sequence of tasks to build something called a Gantt chart. Think of that as a bar graph with tasks laid out in a timeline with the resources needed to get the tasks done.

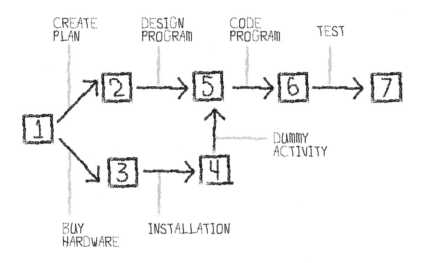

**Figure 9: Sample PERT Chart**

Just before I started working with them, an American giant of a company had make a strategic acquisition and found themselves with a major wireless project for one of the utility companies in London. I came equipped with my PERT and Gantt tools and settled in to develop a detailed project plan. The task list was enormous. A long day later, I had developed a resourced plan that served only to frighten everyone, including me. No one was ready to admit that the project was going to take far longer than anyone wanted. Software-development projects in particular often take longer than expected.

I switched my approach and started to group related tasks together. Some were related by the skill set needed to get them done and others because they were so interdependent. Still other tasks were grouped because they needed access to physical equipment for testing and the like. From this I identified a number of milestones that would make some sense to everyone, especially management. It worked.

The rest of my time at the company was spent persuading management to provide a dedicated space, free pizzas, a huge bonus for completing the milestones on time, and relaxed reporting. In other words, I politely asked them to get out of the way and stop helping quite so much. The results were impressive. The software, hardware, and system engineers decorated their "space" and started burning the midnight oil. The result was a spectacular and timely completion of the project. The customer was ecstatic. The finished project beat the budget and met everyone's requirements.

Another key project-management lesson is to realize that whatever you plan will not unfold as expected. But rather than account for things *not* going as planned, we would rather assume that everything will go well because our project is going to be different. Only it never is, is it? I have found that it helps to divide all task duration estimates by 0.7. The factor is a simple one and spookily accurate. After many years of trying to predict the outcome of complex projects, I learned that we typically lose a little over 40 percent of our effort. It might be vacations or even two vacations or unplanned time off between two people who need to work together. It could be lack of equipment or shipping delays. Or even time for the paint to dry. Yes, I've had that one too!

Somehow, dividing by 0.7 is much more palatable than multiplying by 1.4. It certainly appeared less scary to anyone that figured out the factor, especially management. For one particular company, each product-development task was estimated, grouped into phases that made some sense, and resourced. Each phase was then subject to the magic factor. Guess what? Not a single product-development project was late out of a run of twenty-two separate product-development projects with six phases in each. Every single milestone in each and every phase was completed on time, within budget, and exactly to requirements.

Interestingly, every engineer knew that every known reason for a delay was already taken account of—so no one ever tried making one. There were times when someone worked extra hard, and maybe even a weekend or two was worked from time to time. But no one was assumed to work at full capacity all the time. It was an unreasonable assumption, so it was not made. Instead it was assumed that it would take 40 percent longer than we would like it to, however much we did not like to admit it.

## *Balancing Your Goals*

To this point, we have been focused on chunking down where it is we want to go into individual goals. Where there is, initially at least, no clear end vision, another approach can be helpful. By using this approach from the field of neurolinguistic programming (NLP), it is possible to first develop goals and then extract a "theme" that ultimately leads to a mission and vision. NLP is a way of studying how people excel in any field and teaching these patterns to others. It is modeling mastery in effect. In Steve Andreas's 1994 book *The New Technology of Achievement*, there is a process for developing your own personal goals. It begins by having you develop four lists. The point of the four lists is to build a kind of inventory of goals you would like to achieve.

a)   What you want and already have in your life
b)   What you don't want but have in your life
c)   What you want in your life but do not have
d)   What you do not want in your life and indeed do not have

In the next step you are guided to take something you *don't want in your life but have*, (b), and convert it to something you *don't have but want*. For example, AUBURN had "fear and confusion" that it did not want soon after a series of major mergers and acquisitions. This was converted to a goal for something that was wanted: to build "confidence and clarity."

Next we examine our *want and do not have* list, (c), and our reversed *have and do not want* list, (b). There are usually some recurring themes and a great deal of duplication. The task is to combine the two lists into one and then prioritize them. This is often the stage that evokes a variety of insights. For that reason it is not to be rushed. If multiple departments across a single company performed this exercise, the collated results might suggest a theme involving adding an entirely different range of services or expansion into different markets.

Next we also reverse your *do not want and do not have* list, (d), and turn it into a *want and have* list. The two lists can then be combined and prioritized as with the other two lists. The end result is a single list of all the things that *you have and want* in your life. For example, AUTRON did not have high staff turnover and certainly did not want to lose any of its exceptionally talented engineers. This was converted to a *have and want*—a stable workforce. The exercise is not simply to practice gratitude for all of those things that you *have and want* in your life. It is to ensure that these things that might otherwise be taken for granted are kept in front of your mind. In this example, it provoked a series of promotions and a reward-and-recognition program to maintain the stable workforce.

The world of personal development stresses the importance of balancing goals across different areas of your life and the many different roles that you have.

- financial/income/debt reduction/investments/net worth
- business/professional/career/job

- fun time/recreation/sports/hobbies/travel
- health/fitness/physical
- relationships/family/friends/business
- personal/projects/learning/purchases
- contribution/service/community/legacy
- spirituality

The lesson for the corporate world is to balance goals between departments. During the unprecedented growth at LOFTON, the ambitious growth goals of the four product groups were often not matched in other areas of the business. Adding staff in certain areas was more reactive than it needed to be. The converse was also true. Other departments hired ahead of the growth curve, adding unnecessary expense before it was strictly needed. Often departmental goals are simply rolled up instead of rebalanced.

The final step is to turn the final single list into well-formed goals. So, what is it that constitutes a good goal? One of the keys to achieving goals is to ensure that they are not superficial. Any goal that simply provides instant gratification is unlikely to motivate. The difference between a want and a desire is meaning. There should be a direct link from the goal to the purpose captured in the values, mission, and vision of the individual as well as the enterprise. Tying the goals in this way promotes the passion and drive that ensure that they are achieved. This works especially well with SMART goals. The world of personal development uses SMART goals in the same way that many companies do.

- SIGNIFICANT
  Tiny tasks seldom inspire others to action. Better to leave room for others to fill in the gaps and build their own commitment.

- **M**EANINGFUL
  Passion results from goals tied directly to your purpose and theirs. We are all trying to make a good and lasting difference.

- **A**CTION-ORIENTED
  It is particularly important to have goals that can stimulate action. It is demoralizing to set goals that depend on things largely outside your sphere of influence.

- **R**EWARDING
  Rewards come in all shapes and sizes, but clear feedback on what is working and what is not is the best way to steer your goals in the right direction toward where you want to be.

- **T**RACKABLE
  Though trackable is usually taken to imply adding a timescale, anything that becomes a key performance indicator will improve. It is human nature.

What is done differently as far as goal setting is concerned in the world of personal development compared to most enterprises is to add an additional step. Individuals are taught to use their goals to generate affirmations that are repeated frequently as a means to create cognitive dissonance. Repeatedly stating the goal as though it has already been achieved forces the unconscious mind to look for ways to achieve the goal. For example, a personal goal might be to learn how to "dance the Argentine tango socially by December 31, 2012." An equivalent affirmation is "I am joyful now that I can dance the Argentine tango socially, or something better." Unlike a goal, an affirmation has an emotion attached (joyful, in this case) and assumes that the goal has already been achieved. In an effort not to limit the affirmation, it is typical to add "or something better."

The corporate equivalent relies on the very essence of leadership. If the leaders of an enterprise are constantly showing passion and interest in an outcome, it can have the same effect as affirmations. We all model our behavior on others. If the leaders behave as though something is already so, we will be enrolled and will follow their lead. The leaders at LOFTON were excited about the company's growth goals. They were talked about, planned for, and celebrated constantly by the entire leadership team.

An example set by a leadership team in this way sets up a clear intention. Goals are a way of recording our intentions. Talking about those intentions, or imagining and pretending they have already been achieved, sets up a gap of cognitive dissonance that we each want to close.

No matter how much we plan and prepare and pursue our goals, we have all had our best efforts sabotaged in the most creative of ways. However much commitment, effort, and energy we apply, we have all set goals that we failed to achieve. Though achieving goals helps us feel good, which makes us eager to pursue new challenges, it is not enough. There always seems to be a problem lurking that we could not have foreseen. We so often abandon our goals even though we know they help us take action in the first place, provide focus and a measuring stick, and increase commitment. Why is that? Why do gyms experience such a surge in business right after New Year's only to decline again to previous levels every February? Chapter 6 addresses the limiting beliefs that plague our efforts and sabotage our best intentions.

Chapter Six

# Removing Obstacles:
# Overcoming the Inevitable Sabotage

> Each of us has an unconscious tendency to trip our
> upper limit switch, and each of us can eliminate
> that tendency. We deserve to experience wave after
> wave of greater love, creative energy, and financial
> abundance, without the compulsion
> to sabotage ourselves.
> —Gay Hendricks, *The Big Leap: Conquer Your*
> *Hidden Fear and Take Life to the Next Level*

Having set a clear intention of how we want to *be* to get us where we want to go and having chunked it down to specific (SMART) goals, we may still experience failure. Our best efforts are often sabotaged. There is often some insurmountable obstacle to achieving our goal. This chapter is about removing those obstacles. By obstacles we mean things that get in the way and prevent that which we intended to *be* from happening. There are several reasons why the goals we set are not always achieved. There are times when we simply need to modify our goals based on what we've learned along the way. We have mentioned the need to remain open. Often when pursuing a goal, we learn more and better ways to accomplish the same end. In these cases, we simply make necessary adjustments and continue on our merry way. This is a normal, in fact, essential process. But even then, there are times when we still fail to achieve our goals.

So in what ways do we fail to achieve our corporate goals?

- failure to follow change-management best practices
- unanticipated external effect
- unanticipated side effect
- change exceeds the corporation's capacity for change
- insufficient cost/benefit
- resistance from an unseen limiting belief
- change not for the greatest good of all
- weak to nonexistent commitment to change

Let us take a look at each of these in turn.


## Change Management

Whether we pursue a single goal or a complex arrangement of many interrelated goals, each one invariably creates some level of change. One of the reasons why we might fail to accomplish our goal or goals is that we ignore the best practices from the established field of change management. The research behind the change-management industry has proposed many models of change over the past thirty years. And while there are myriad models of change management, no single model seems to quite capture it all. However, there are certainly some best practices that have stood the test of time. Most of these are known and understood by many executives. Essentially, it has been shown that change projects improve their chances of success when they have the following characteristics:

a) **Corporate Sponsors**
One or more corporate sponsors visibly support and model the change.

b) **Resourcing**
The change is adequately resourced by the best available talent.

c) **Engagement**
Everyone affected by the change is engaged in the process of change.

d) **Communication**
The compelling reason for the change, the process of change, the lessons learned, and the benefits of the outcomes are continually communicated.

e) **Chunking**
Change is chunked down into phases that can be delivered quickly to demonstrate incremental success.

f) **Underpinning**
The changes are underpinned.

a) **Corporate Sponsors.** You are probably very aware of the significant role played by senior executives in the success of any large-scale corporate change effort. Having highly visible corporate sponsorship is paramount to successful corporate change. At SIPTON, I observed a very remarkable effect. The average of all of the DiSC profiles of the employees in the office in New York was identical to the DiSC profile of the president of that office. The average of all of the DiSC profiles of the employees in the San Diego office matched that of the president of that office. Yet individual DiSC profiles varied as much as they would in any company. There seems to be more at play here than restricted hiring practices. In fact, many times the culture of a whole company or some subdivision is modeled on its established leader. Because one of the most predominant ways we learn is by modeling others, the example set by the leader, particularly when showing a new way to *be*, will have a significant impact.

b) **Resourcing.** Another key success factor in all change efforts is adequate resourcing. We often feel compelled to keep our most valued resources doing what they are doing (since they are obviously "doing it right") while populating new initiatives with less essential and often less talented team members. Then we wonder why our efforts fail.

c) **Engagement.** Best practice in change management also demands that everyone affected by the change is fully engaged in the process of change. A common mistake is to believe that simply providing some rationale for a given change will obtain the necessary buy-in to that change. Indeed, some kind of rationale is absolutely essential for many people who value steadiness and predictability. But those who more readily embrace change are typically less interested in reasons. These people want to be involved in *driving* the change. They are open to change as long as it is not being done to them. These are the individuals usually identified as change agents. So, providing a rationale is a good start, but it is not enough to achieve buy-in for everyone.

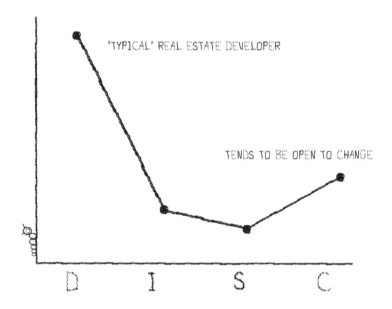

**Figure 10: DiSC Profile—Open to Change**

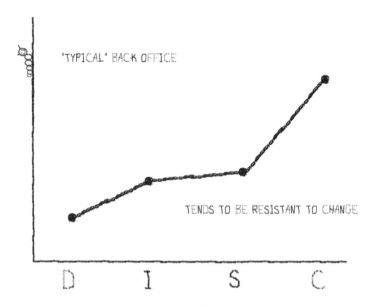

**Figure 11: DiSC Profile—Resistant to Change**

A phrase used often to convey the reason for a change is the burning platform. If a platform is on fire, there is a compelling reason to move away from it. However, only about half of the population is more negatively motivated; they are driven *away from* something that is bad for them. The other half of the population is more positively motivated. These people need something positive and beneficial to move *toward*. The best change efforts provide both something to move away from and something else to move toward.

However, even if we provide a reason to move away from how things are and a benefit to move to something different, it is still not always enough to achieve buy-in for everyone. Buy-in requires engagement. People have different motivations and so need to align a proposed change with something that is valued by them. The change must appeal to something that is important to them; otherwise they will consciously or unconsciously sabotage the change effort. Buy-in is a process of individually enrolling people.

d) **Communication.** Enrollment demands continual communication of the compelling reason for a change, the process of change itself, the lessons learned on the way, and the ultimate benefits of the outcomes. When change management became an industry in its own right, it started to productize what is essentially a process. Communicating upbeat messages about how well the project is progressing is unlikely to promote any kind of engagement. At LOFTON, my own efforts to repeat the benefits of moving to a new database-management platform in a regular newsletter were well intentioned but failed. The process of change requires interaction. What I had failed to understand was that resistance was a necessary precondition for any kind of enrollment. Had I listened more to the resistance I might have been able to find a better match between the technology and a real business need.

e) **Chunking.** Chunking down a project into phases that can be delivered quickly helps to demonstrate success. We have already addressed the considerable benefits to chunking down our problem in the previous chapter. A succession of accomplishments quickly teaches the benefits of the effort and accelerates enrollment. A company, like an individual, is liable to lose interest over time without interim milestones. Both as individuals and as evolving enterprises, we learn through repetition.

f) **Underpinning.** The final best practice from the world of change management is to lock in results. I use the word "underpin" to mean securing the change in stages so as not to risk slipping back into old patterns. New Year's resolutions fail because of the predominance of what we are used to. We tend to fall back to our comfort zone. Change is unfamiliar, uncomfortable, and more than a little scary. We must first learn, through practice, to become consciously competent in some new way. Unless this new habit is protected in some way, we risk never making it to unconsciously competent. If we do not lock in the new habit so that it is performed unconsciously, our old patterns will simply reemerge. We will inevitably slip back to our old way of being.

So the first of the reasons why we fail to achieve our corporate goals is that we often attempt to implement them without following the best practices of change management. If a business is to grow and develop, it must consciously evaluate its failed goals against these current best practices. Anything less is likely to teach the culture an unintended lesson that will ultimately sabotage its future efforts. But even adhering to all of the accepted best practices of change management will not guarantee that all of our goals will be achieved. There will always be external effects that cannot be anticipated.

## Surprise Surprise

On a fairly regular basis, something happens that really could not have been foreseen. This category is not intended as a way to excuse poor planning or basic risk management. But despite our best efforts, sometimes things happen that cannot be accommodated by adjusting our goal or resetting our intention. They take us by complete surprise. What is most interesting is that in the corporate world as much as the personal-development field, we stay in denial for way too long after we have been surprised. Somehow we convince ourselves that this external effect will go away and that if we just push on harder and longer we will somehow break through and achieve our goal.

It is of far more benefit to the enterprise to stop and consider the effect of the external event. Has it simply exposed one of the other ways in which we fail to achieve our goals? Has the event highlighted a weakness in our change-management methodology, provoked a damaging side effect that we could not have foreseen, or perhaps just been one change too many? Maybe the cost in effort is simply not warranted. Has some previous experience left us with a belief that makes the goal unachievable? Perhaps the goal is not in everyone's best interest? Or is it simply that we were never that committed to the goal in the first place? If it is none of these, then it could simply be some external effect that we could not have anticipated.

If there is no way in which we could know or expect the event, then the way in which we handle it provides a significant learning opportunity. We have eliminated the possibility that we can adjust our goal, so we must abandon it. AUTRON recognized that it had missed its window of opportunity and had insufficient resources to make the technological leap to regain its former position as provider of the fastest product in its field. Its initial failure to acknowledge that reality almost cost the company its very survival. At the very first moment a company is surprised, it is time to review its goals, abandon those that can no longer be achieved, and learn from the experience.

However, there are occasions when a goal fails, not because of some effect on the goal itself but because of an unwanted side effect that it creates.

## *The Unexpected*

There is some interesting research that addresses what happens when a company experiences an unexpected side effect to an initiative. If the side effect provides an unexpected benefit, the leader of the business is not given credit for the outcome. It is said that she was just in the right place at the right time. However, if the unanticipated side effect has a negative outcome, that same executive gets the blame.

An unfortunate effect of this phenomenon is a failure to learn the lesson offered. Let me explain. One of the ways in which we deal with failure is to assign blame. Once we have identified a culpable victim, the learning stops. In a number of high-profile instances recently, one or more executives have been held responsible for the unanticipated side effect of a complete collapse of an enterprise. The moment someone is to blame, the work to find the flaws in the system that permitted such a failure are typically either abandoned or treated with less urgency.

If failure to accomplish a goal is due to an unexpected side effect, then there is a valuable lesson to be learned. Finding one or more individuals to blame is akin to treating a symptom. Remaining curious and looking for the root cause will strengthen the enterprise. But please note that unanticipated side effects all provide opportunities for a lesson—whether there is a negative or a positive outcome. Both should be studied. Even if we learn our lessons well it is possible that we simply need a rest. Just one goal too many can leave us exhausted.

## *Initiative Fatigue*

As one might expect, with the title of senior vice president of change management comes a certain license to change things. Indeed, anything less than a full portfolio of change initiatives might be considered poor performance. During my time at LOFTON, when I held just such a title, I saw it as my responsibility to perpetually identify challenges and opportunities that would require a change initiative to address. There was never a shortage.

Over a period of three years amidst a background of unprecedented growth, there were ten to twelve major change initiatives in process at any given time. Until one day, one of the senior executives coined the phrase "initiative fatigue." Once it had a label, it was quickly adopted as a mantra for my fellow overworked and overwhelmed senior executives.

At first I was shocked and dismayed. Could my colleagues not appreciate that we needed to sustain this pace of change to keep up with our own growth? If we slowed now it would curb our growth. Though when I stopped to consider the pattern of changes over the three years, there had been change upon change. There were no periods to monitor and reflect. No time had been set aside to measure what had changed and consider its effectiveness.

One of the significant lessons learned in the field of personal development is the need to consolidate what has been learned. Any human goes through cycles quite naturally. After a period of change and growth, a period of time to practice what has been learned is a requirement. Even on a weight-loss program it is well understood that there will be periods where the body simply stops losing weight for a while, even though the calorie intake and exercise regimen is unchanged. To reach a plateau before embarking on further change is a natural and much-needed phenomenon.

Even in a company with a culture that is open to high levels of change, there must be periods of consolidation. Recall that even if the overall culture displays openness to it, there will always be those individuals within the culture who cannot handle perpetual change. Not only do occasional plateaus help these individuals assimilate change, but the time can be usefully used to measure and communicate its benefit to help ensure that the culture has learned the right lesson and to underpin the changes. Taking stock is the best way to allow the culture to learn the right lessons consciously.

### Not Worth It

SIPTON had experienced painfully high attrition. More than 70 percent of the employees in a given year either quit or were fired. One of the consequences was a distinct lack of corporate learning. Each new hopeful employee would add to the company's archived documentation based on their own limited view of what should be kept and how it should be organized. Over a period of fifty years, the results were frightening. The organization had vacillated from keeping everything to destroying important records. The ultimate result was a set of over seven hundred boxes of information without rhyme or reason.

A project was launched to bring sense and order to the archive so that it would be easy to find any given piece of information. It quickly became apparent, however, that the work required to organize the documents greatly outweighed any benefit that might accrue. It was simply not worth the effort, so the goal was modified.

Recall the concept of the burning platform. It is the compelling reason why a project or goal is being undertaken. It is imperative that everyone jumps off the burning platform. The problem of developing deeply convincing and logical reasons to take on one or more goals is that we can blind ourselves to the reality that it is just not worth it. The lesson to be learned here is the need to put aside the burning platform and consider whether the benefit significantly outweighs the effort, irrespective of the strength of the reason for doing it. Even then we may still find that some unseen force sabotages our most beneficial goals. It is as though there is some hidden limiting belief.

## The Unconscious Saboteur

A very smart and insightful friend sent me *The Big Leap—Conquer Your Hidden Fear and Take Life to the Next Level* by Gay Hendricks (2009). The book addresses how early life experiences leave us with limiting beliefs. These limiting beliefs later conspire to form a glass ceiling, which the book calls the *upper limit switch*, causing us to self-sabotage. When we are most successful in business or most in love or feeling abundant, we feel unworthy and sabotage our efforts in the most creative ways.

A number of things stood out to me in the book:

- Many of our fears are based on the workings of the ego, the part of us that's focused on getting recognition and protecting us from social ostracism.
- Each of us has an unconscious tendency to trip our upper limit switch, and each of us can eliminate that tendency and remove the compulsion to sabotage ourselves.
- By age forty, many of us have tuned out our "call to genius" and are getting loud, repeated alarms hidden in the form of depression, illness, injuries, and relationship conflict.
- The art of getting beyond our upper limit has a lot to do with creating space within us to feel and appreciate natural good feelings. By natural I mean good feelings that aren't induced by alcohol, sugar, and other short-term fixes.
- When you suffer symptoms of illness or experience an accident, you often do so because you're unconsciously trying to prevent yourself from having to do something you don't really want to do and/or protect yourself from something you don't want to feel.
- Upper limit behaviors include getting sick or hurt, hiding significant feelings, and not speaking significant truths to relevant people.
- Stress and conflict are caused by resisting acceptance and ownership. If there is any part of ourselves or our lives that we're not fully willing to accept, we will experience stress and friction in that area.
- It's the act of stifling and concealing feelings that causes problems in relationships.

In other words, the problem sometimes lies with the unconscious things that sabotage our best efforts. How do we handle them in the world of personal development? There are a plethora of techniques. All of them work to bring what is unconscious to the conscious mind. Unfortunately, some therapies stop at this point and fail to replace the errant obstacle with something else—a different thought, attitude, value, belief, or behavior. The most helpful insight is from the field of NLP. After having hit the obstruction that has derailed your goal, the first step is to acknowledge that's what it is. The next step is to identify or evaluate the unconscious belief that tripped you up. The final step is to make a behavior or attitude change and underpin the change through repetition and accountability. Sounds easy, huh?

The equivalent approach for a business also sounds pretty easy but is one of the hardest things to do. The process starts with collectively examining how this errant belief may have been adopted in the first place so you can build a shared understanding of where it came from. Then, by working together, it is possible to reach a shared understanding of what you want to believe or value or what attitude or behavior you decide to adopt in its place in the future. Finally, by establishing structures, policies, and metrics the change can be reinforced. But none of these techniques will work if the goal or change is not what we might call "ecological."

### Greater Good

Those on a spiritual journey seeking their own enlightenment pursue a path of increasing awareness. A business enterprise might not see itself on anything like a spiritual journey, but it is helpful to view it as such. Like any individual, a company is growing and developing. So, interestingly, another way to view all of the myriad ways that our efforts to achieve a given goal are sabotaged is as feedback that can support the process of growth and development. Whatever obstruction is met provides information that could be used to further the growth and development of our enterprise.

Every one of the eight ways we fail to achieve our corporate goals presented here provides an opportunity to learn and grow. The question is whether you will learn from the failure consciously or unconsciously. If you fail to review outcomes, then the enterprise will simply draw its own conclusions unconsciously. Beliefs and attitudes will be modified, whether intentionally or not.

The goal that is not achieved because it is not for the greatest good of all is probably the one most difficult to understand. But a goal will fail if it is not in the best interests of all. In other words the goal must be ecological. NLP relies upon a step in its various change techniques to judge whether a given change is ecological. Questions are asked about a goal to make sure the outcome fits within all aspects of your life:

- What is the *real* purpose of the goal?
- What will I lose or gain if I have it?
- What will happen if I get it?
- What won't happen if I get it?
- What will happen if I don't get it?
- What won't happen if I don't get it?

The observant reader will note that these questions are similar to the example of inquiry (from quantum linguistics) introduced in chapter 2. The whole idea of conscious inquiry applies equally to learning from failed goals as much as the establishment of goals in the first instance. Consciously exploring a goal in this way helps ensure that it truly is for the greater good of all. Most people will resist a goal that will result in a change that they perceive as not in everyone's best interest. As we have learned, resistance to change can show up in the most creative of ways.

Addressing this particular way in which we fail to achieve our goals relates directly to one of the best practices of change management—that of communication. It is vital to clearly demonstrate how and why a given goal is for the greater good. If it is not, it really should not be sought.

## *Lacking Intention*

Assuming that we have become clear about where it is we want to go, how is it that we might lack the intention to achieve our goal? We identified the goal as a sure way of helping us achieve our ultimate vision. The world of self-development identifies four steps to achieving intentions. Intentions work best by first getting clear about them, then enrolling the support of others, next constantly working on them, and finally celebrating their achievement. While all these steps are absolutely essential, what most commonly sabotages our intentions is not having really made the initial decision.

Let me explain.

One of the hardest lessons to digest in the world of personal transformation is that it is our choices that have brought us to where we are at this moment in time. Once we have become upset or disgusted enough about where we are at the moment, we start to feel the motivation to do something about it. In that process we might consciously decide to make a change. We develop one or more goals that will take us toward where it is we want to be. But it is our unconscious beliefs that have not changed. We are not yet congruent in our decision to make a change.

In Robert MacPhee's 2010 book, *Manifesting for Non-Gurus—How to Quickly and Easily Attract Lasting Results*, he presents the self-fulfilling prophecy. We are constantly working (unconsciously) to get our results into a comfort zone. Our actions produce our results. It is our thoughts, perhaps driven and modified by external influences, that drive our actions. And it is the self-talk dialogue between our thoughts and our beliefs that often unconsciously impact our thoughts. This negatively affects our actions and in turn sabotages our results. All of which ultimately leads us right back to our comfort zone.

So how can we form a clear intention? We must discover those things that sabotage our efforts and *consciously* address them. An individual struggling with relationships eventually identifies one or more repeating patterns. Underneath a pattern is one or more limiting beliefs. In exactly the same way, a company has limiting beliefs that cause it to repeat certain patterns of behavior. The question to be asked repeatedly is "What must the business believe in order for it to behave in this way?" If that particular belief limits outcomes, then it needs to be openly considered and, if necessary, revised.

Recall that AUTRON believed that it was a start-up whose purpose was to supply the world with its fastest available computer. At its launch, AUTRON's technology was well in advance of the market. By leveraging the resources of a large American distributor, AUTRON had positioned itself well. However, the extended due diligence of a potential acquirer distracted AUTRON to the point where it fell hopelessly behind in the technology race. Left with mounting debt and no sales, Managers and employees alike at AUTRON still held firmly to the belief that somehow the firm would recover and once again have the fastest computer in the world. The American distributor returned the now obsolete computers, the bailiffs arrived at the door to collect assets, and still they held doggedly to their belief. Only when they were able to

consciously address their reality were they able to move
forward.

## *Alignment*

Note that every single one of the eight reasons listed for failure
to achieve our goals is somehow linked to learning:

- **Change Management**
  The entire field of change management is an attempt
  to learn from common mistakes made and present
  best practices for others to follow.

- **Surprise Surprise and the Unexpected**
  Both positive and negative side effects of a change
  provide learning opportunities in the same way as an
  unanticipated surprise event.

- **Initiative Fatigue**
  When there has been one too many goals pursued, it
  provides pause to move from *consciously competent* to
  *unconsciously competent* to reinforce learning.

- **Not Worth It and Greater Good**
  It is impossible not to learn something of value when
  examining whether a given goal is beneficial (worth it)
  or ecological (for the greater good).

- **The Unconscious Saboteur**
  The most common reason for failure of any goal due
  to an unconscious belief provides the most significant
  lesson, whether for the individual or the company.

- **Lacking Intention**
  Finally, getting clear about an intention is the surest way of learning what might sabotage our efforts before they even begin.

If change is learning, then to change is to grow and develop. No one said growth and development had to mean always moving in the same direction, now did they? But how is it that we can generally move forward and grow without going too far off course and causing the entire business to fail? The answer lies in constantly seeking a level of realignment.

One of the ways by which we can view any given change is to consider different levels, or aspects. Typically we use this kind of model to move from detail to a more abstracted view of something. Maybe this just appeals to my background as an engineer, but it may help explain how this realignment process works. If we model the levels or aspects of an individual, we might show identity at the top, then beliefs or values, thoughts, behaviors, and finally the environment. You have doubtless experienced what happens when you have an underlying belief that is different from a thought you are having. The thought leads to some new behavior. But the new behavior is soon sabotaged, because it is out of alignment with your beliefs.

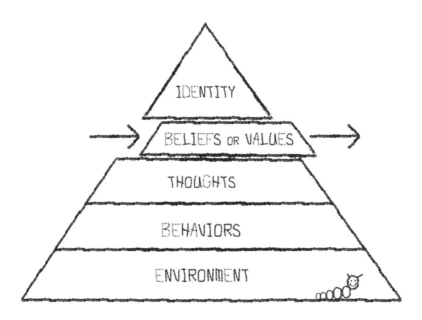

**Figure 12: Identity—Environment**

For a company, we might use a similar model and put mission—our identity as a business—at the top. Our beliefs and values are caught up in our culture. Next are the goals we use to direct our efforts, which in turn produce our results. Our results interact with our market. Similar to the example of an individual is what happens when there is notable misalignment between, say, the company's goals and its mission (its identity or purpose).

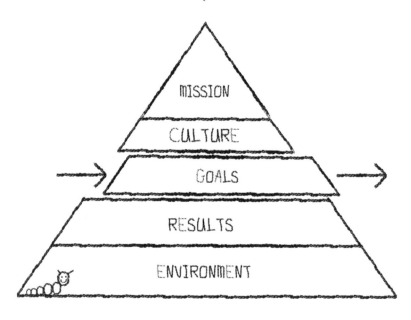

**Figure 13: Mission—Market**

Change inevitably causes some misalignment. The solution to this dilemma is to promote a shift in as many different aspects as possible so that they all reach realignment at the same time. Many individuals believe that they simply have to have a new thought to change a habit. Yet we see over and over that this does not work. A single errant belief will sabotage our best efforts. Many companies believe that they can throw up a new goal that is someone's pet aim. It never works. Unless everything is coherent it invariably backfires. Is it really that simple? Yes, it is. Coherence, or alignment, is what makes us comfortable (again) so we can underpin the change we have made and prepare to change some more.

This does not imply some unseen limit on the stretch we can achieve with a new goal. The gap between where you are and where you want to be has only to be believable. But it is important to keep everything in alignment and address our mission, values and beliefs, our culture, our goals, and the needs of our market. Even then we could use a little help. Willpower alone is not enough. We now turn to our much-needed help.

## Chapter Seven

# Much-Needed Help: Vital Support to Get Where You Want to Go

> While the benefits of masterminding with people outside your field may not seem obvious now, the truth is we all tend to get "stuck" in our own field of expertise, doing things the same way everyone else in our industry does. But when you assemble people from different industries and professions, you get lots of different perspectives on the same subject.
> —Jack Canfield, *The Success Principles*

Perhaps now we are clear about where it is we are headed. Maybe we have even broken our vision down to manageable changes. One of the main ways that we tackle the unavoidable obstacles on the way is to recruit the help of others. Most of us appreciate that we need help. It can sometimes be the only way to step out of our own conditioning to see things as they really are. But those closest to us whom we rely upon for that essential help may actually get in the way of our attempts to change. Even assuming we have followed every possible guideline and all levels of our effort to change have been perfectly aligned, we may yet discover that our "help" is actually a hindrance. We invest time and effort in building relationships with those we feel will support our efforts. The very help that we have recruited ends up being the cause of our failure. Why is that?

## *Accountability*

It is important to tell others about your intentions. Having someone else hold you accountable for something you said you were going to do is generally one of the surest ways of getting it accomplished. This process works equally well personally and in a corporation. The more people that are told about the change that is to be made, the better the chances of success. The controller at SIPTON had developed a habit where if she was disturbed when working intensively on a task she would keep working, avoid eye contact, and use only enough words to make it clear the interruption was unwelcomed. She decided that she wanted to change that habit and be open and welcoming to her team and others at all times. Following the annual 360°-review process, she informed the staff of her intention. Everyone enjoyed trying to catch her practicing her old ways. She quickly made a measurable change in habit.

So what is accountability? It is recognizing that if you are busy being part of the problem, you are probably in the victim cycle. The first step is to gain sufficient awareness to get out. Then you assume responsibility and move to take action. There is a fabulous set of three books, the Oz Series, that travels deeply into the subject of accountability (Partners in Leadership 1994). The three books, *The Oz Principle, Change the Culture, Change the Game,* and *How Did That Happen?,* focus respectively on the importance of individuals taking accountability for results, teams sharing accountability, and the ways to evoke accountability in others. Having someone else help you stay accountable is effectively recruiting someone to catch you slipping into the victim cycle. Usually pointing out that you are busier blaming others than taking action is enough to help you out of the victim cycle.

It seems as though we find it easier to let ourselves off the hook than to let someone else down. So sharing your intentions to change recruits others into helping you stay personally accountable and out of the victim cycle. But if telling one friend or colleague of your desire to change is helpful, it stands to reason that telling more people would be even better. Well, it can be. If we make our corporate aim public, then we will be subject to public scrutiny. Clearly, it must be done with care, as the public can be a harsh and unforgiving judge. There is a great reluctance to abandon a change that many others know about simply because it is difficult or because it has been sabotaged by the hidden unconscious beliefs of the enterprise. These are quickly exposed. It is much easier to make more effort to effect the change than it is to tolerate public ridicule. When properly harnessed, peer pressure is a powerful tool.

When INSOL became a public company, it announced that it was the world leader in its chosen field. It built its entire brand around being the world leader in high-integrity systems. When threatened by other technologies, it quickly responded by acquiring more. The initial claims did much to shift the perception of customers and competitors alike that INSOL was indeed a world leader. When it faced a challenge to that position, it responded quickly to reclaim its position.

Corporate branding is different from product branding. Where product branding can be seen as aligning an image of a product with a market need or preference, corporate branding is creating an image of the culture or style of an entire enterprise. The very essence of powerful corporate branding is to align the style of the business with its messaging. Making public an intention to change creates the same kind of cognitive dissonance that drives an individual to change. When AUBURN publically announced it was now number two in its field, it was not about to let anyone overtake it.

When AUTRON announced it was known for its reliability, it was not about to demonstrate any kind of unreliable behavior. When INSOL informed everyone that it was the clear leader in its field, it was not easily going to give that leadership position up.

The world of personal development strongly recommends this form of accountability to support your efforts to get where you want to be. Ever since the concept was introduced to me during Jack Canfield's "Train the Trainer" course, I have worked with an accountability buddy. Stephen and I share our goals on a weekly basis. Over several years it still is somewhat surprising—and very effective—that neither of us wants to let the other down. It is much easier to make the extra effort to get a change accomplished than it is to hear the disappointment in Stephen's voice when I fall short. I will do almost anything to avoid that knowing groan. He certainly now knows me better than I pretend to know myself.

During the recent Great Recession, Stephen shunned the negativity rife in his own country (Ireland) and elected instead to prepare his enterprise for substantial growth. At a time when everyone else was shrinking, Stephen was doubling his staff, building essential infrastructure, and opening new international offices. All of his efforts culminated in a very public opening of his new premises. The national dignitaries attending and the strength of his message attracted the media. Stephen, normally the shy type, proudly made his pledge to create new jobs to fuel the much-needed economic recovery. Standing up and very publically declaring his intention was something that Stephen previously would have avoided. He had changed and must continue to change. His company will need to change as it grows and develops, so Stephen will need to continue to change and develop as well. Now that his intention to change is out there, I am sure that Stephen will do whatever it takes to achieve his own goals and those of his business. Even if that means I get to remind him every once in a while!

In the simplest case, we tell a friend or colleague of our intention to make a change. Consciously, at least, they seem keen to support our desire and offer whatever help we say we need to get to where we want to be. But everyone is constantly looking for a comfortable state. Part of that need causes us to assign roles and responsibilities to those closest to us. We have a particular role or set of expectations for all our friends and colleagues. When they move outside of their assigned role, we often unconsciously and very subtly bring them back into line with our expectations of them. While our friend or colleague intellectually supports the change, they unconsciously need us to continue to perform to their original expectations of us. If there is a clash, then they will unwittingly sabotage our efforts to change and keep us in the role to which they have become accustomed. Would it help to use a different structure to reduce the effect of someone else's expectations of us?

## *Masterminding*

An extension of the idea of an accountability partner is particularly valuable to business leaders. The world of personal development promotes relying on a mastermind group to stay accountable. A mastermind group is a very disparate group of professionals who are already at the level you aspire to. The purpose of the group is to bring insights that help you break out of your current mind-set and see things in a very different way. It helps bring out unconscious beliefs that may be holding you back. The group will quickly identify you in a victim cycle and bring it to your attention. A mastermind group provides access to other resources beyond your own circle of friends and colleagues.

It is usual for such a group to stay together for some time, so members get to know each other very well. Such groups might meet for one or two hours at a time once or twice a month, typically by phone or videoconference. Over time, each member comes to learn the recurring and persistent patterns of behavior of the other members. Though it might seem unlikely, the effect of *not* having the time to get lost in the details or be from the same industry is the *advantage*. Patterns are easier to identify when you have a very different outlook and experience. Not being personal friends also permits each member to be completely frank and honest. There is no close friendship at stake. For a mastermind group to be successful, the organizer should follow these guidelines:

- Choose people who are already where you want to be.
- Choose people who are from different professional arenas.
- Choose people who can introduce you to a network.
- Hold meetings at least every other week.
- Hold the meetings in person, if possible.
- Strictly manage meetings to be only one hour in duration.
- Assign a timekeeper.
- First meetings should be used for one participant to familiarize others with his or her situation, needs, and challenges.
- Open with a simple invocation.
- Share what is new and good.
- Negotiate for time slots.
- Individual member speaks while others brainstorm solutions.
- Each participant makes a commitment to accomplish something before the next meeting.
- End with gratitude.

You might well ask: Why would those in positions that I aspire to join my mastermind group? Interestingly, just because you are asking is enough for some people to want to contribute. Leaders of organizations really do have a lonely role. A chance to learn from their peers in a safe forum is attractive. It works. It is also a very powerful way to reduce the likelihood of an individual accountability partner becoming an obstacle. But even then you will experience resistance to any change.

## *Resistance*

Relying on a friend or colleague, making a very public announcement of your brand through your messaging, or even having an entire mastermind group hold you accountable still might not be enough. The kind and degree of help and support that you need really depends upon the kind and degree of change you are undertaking. It seems fairly intuitive that you will not get needed support from someone who is negatively affected or even just threatened by your planned change. Maybe you can only count on such support from those who somehow benefit from the change.

The first thing to consider of the friend or colleague is the strength and intent of the resistance directed at the change. If the real underlying intent of the resistance is constructive, then the change or goal can be adjusted. Everybody wins. It is really interesting that resistance in the field of change management is most often assumed to be negative. LOFTON launched its major automation project, making a considerable investment in new software. Owner expectations were so high that the project had to be severely slimmed down in a vain attempt to accomplish anything at all before everyone's patience expired. Even then, the project failed to meet enough of anyone's expectations to garner support. It was abandoned. The write-off was huge. Instead of using it to learn (a very expensive) lesson, it was never talked about. By now the reader might be thinking about the unconscious belief that this experience left behind.

Because the feedback is unwelcomed does *not* mean it is incorrect. It should have been immediately clear at LOFTON that the company had no patience for a long-term solution. Very configurable software might best grow with the company but would take too much time and effort to achieve anything useful. It would have been far better to start small and solve some immediate needs with a more standard software product. It is not just that hindsight wisdom is a wonderful thing; the feedback at the start of the project should have been enough to highlight the strategic error before the investment was made.

So often the resistance is constructive but delivered with such ferocity that it at least damages if not destroys the entire project. Any project needs nurturing at first. Even if its direction should be adjusted, it should be done with great care. Others threatened by the proposed change are only too quick to jump on board and use the constructive resistance to win their case that the initiative should be abandoned.

Consider if the change or goal is a ball and the constructive resistance is some contact with the ball. The ball, traveling at speed, can have its path changed by gently knocking it on the side until it goes where you want it to go. But if the ball has not built up enough speed, then almost any kind of adjustment is likely to bring it to a standstill. Standing in front of the ball will certainly affect the path of the ball. Either it will just stop, causing a great deal of pain in the process, or it will vector off in an unanticipated direction.

What is to be done if the resistance is not constructive? It is likely that the motive for the resistance is at least questionable.

Assuming we have created a safe place, then we could turn to the same questioning techniques introduced in chapter 2 to get to the real motivation. It should quickly become apparent if the resistance is based on perhaps a fear of loss.

Charlie had been the fix-it guy for everything IT related. He also enjoyed having his one staff member. He was slowly building his own ability to delegate and took great pride in the growth and development of his apprentice. When his apprentice moved on to bigger and better things, the company decided to outsource all desktop and server support instead of building up an IT team. What was initially a welcomed idea was soon strongly resisted. Charlie's fear crept in and dominated his thinking for a while. It took reassurance and encouragement for him to move into his new role as master facilitator and leave behind his fear of loss.

It should be stressed that any form of overt resistance is still preferred to passive-aggressive behavior. Once you know that there is resistance, you can set to work to determine if it is constructive or destructive. If it is constructive, the change or goal can be adjusted accordingly. Destructive resistance can be confronted in an attempt to negate its effect. In either case, the next step is enrollment.

### *Enrollment*

In this sense, enrollment is a kind of joining as with joining a course of study. The field of change management refers to this function as *getting buy-in*. The difficulty with this description of the process is that it implies that others have to give something up in order to buy-in to a change. Enrollment is more about what someone else gains. The process of enrollment is about sharing with others what everyone will gain once they are enrolled.

Enrolling relies upon building a relationship. That relationship begins by identifying mutually satisfying benefits from a proposed change. That change must in some way help the enrollee meet their goals and avoid their predominant fears. The communication must be based on adequate rapport. Finally, the enroller must deliver on the promises made.

The announcements of change initiatives often begin with

- this is why I am doing it,
- this is why we should do it,
- this is why you should change, or
- this is why it should be done.

The only way to enroll anyone into anything begins with

- this is how you benefit.

If you are unable to identify some benefit, you really have no business attempting to enroll someone in the change. If the company is trying to put a spin on a questionable change, everyone in the organization will see through it immediately and it will fail. I learned a most unfortunate phrase early in my career. It went something like "How do you get turkeys to vote for Thanksgiving?" The answer is, you don't. If there is nothing in it for them, the change should be either modified or abandoned. Of course, that raises the question of how we handle changes like downsizing. The answer to that is to amend the change to incorporate sufficient benefits such that everybody gets something out of the change.

Too often the decision to downsize is based on a false premise. If the real motivation is simply to cut costs to increase profits in the short term, it usually backfires in the long run. The revenues collapse and the company starts to chase the revenues down by more and more waves of layoffs.

If the company is not profitable, it could be that its lack of profitability means that it cannot attract sufficient investment to adapt to changes in its marketplace. If this is presented as the reason for change, it is far more likely to enroll employees in the initiative, even if it ultimately means that some of them will lose their jobs. It demands real communication about the real reason with a real plan and a real commitment to see it through to the end. It must include a plan to attract and make the necessary investment to secure its future.

Even with a change that will provide a real benefit to the enterprise, there is still a need to enroll employees individually in the change. The reason is that everyone is different. One obvious difference is individuals' communication preferences. Unless the change is presented in writing, orally, and perhaps even graphically, the message will not even be received by everyone. Let us assume that the change does provide a series of real benefits and we have developed a rich communication plan to explain the change and the various benefits. Some estimate that up to 70 percent of employees in such a change will accept the rationale and work cooperatively to implement that change. The benefit is clear to them.

The situation is absolutely no different when enrolling friends and colleagues to support your planned change. If you use their preferred communication style, then up to 70 percent of those you attempt to enroll will recognize the benefit to them and support your efforts. That leaves at least 30 percent who might not be supportive. This, even though there *is* a benefit to them and it has been communicated. Why is it that so many refuse to recognize the benefit and support the change? Well, the change needs to be communicated in a way that will enroll them in the change.

The next level of communication should be matched to the prevailing style of the whole group. Using the DiSC behavioral-modeling tool, it is possible to identify the likely behavioral patterns of the whole culture of the enterprise. SIPTON's headquarters staff was predominantly high "C." One important characteristic behavior of high "Cs" is that they are very private and will not readily divulge information about how they feel about a planned change. Consequently, it was difficult to judge their level of enrollment in the proposed change. But the one thing most highly prized by such a culture is correctness. Making the "single source of truth" a core element of the change enrolled most. Being reliable further developed trust, keeping the project on time and ensuring that standards of quality were maintained, and enrolled the majority of the staff. The scope of the change and the way it was communicated was engineered to provide the maximum benefit and address the fears and motivations of the majority. Still there were individuals who were not enrolled in the change.

The process of enrollment has much to do with communication, but it is not so much telling as connecting. The commercial real estate industry specifically describes the chief administrative officer (CAO) as one who leads shared services, typically including marketing, IT, and HR. The power of the role is its ability to drive strategic change. Marketing can be used to announce the change, HR to coach everyone in the new way of being so as to enroll everyone in the change, and IT to underpin the change, perhaps through automating processes. But there will always be those individuals who need to hear the rationale for the change in terms they understand if they are to be enrolled.

## *Adapting*

The commercial real estate industry is populated with many individuals with the *Creative* DiSC behavior pattern.

Their primary goal is dominance, and their greatest fear is lack of influence. They bring value to the organization by initiating changes. Attempting to enroll a *Creative* pattern by emphasizing the "single source of truth" or explaining how the change will help to ensure that information will be correct will never be enough. The best way to enroll a *Creative* pattern in a given change is to let them lead at least some aspect of the change. Make them responsible for initiating the change. Make it their idea.

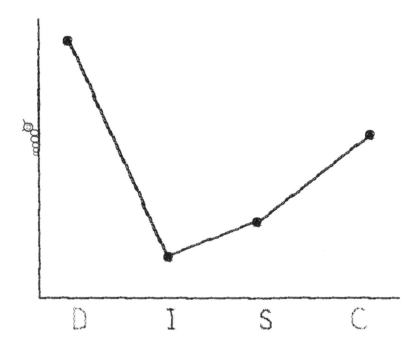

**Figure 14: Creative Pattern DiSC Profile**

The greatest struggle for someone with a *Creative* pattern is dealing with someone with a High-S, such as the *Investigator* pattern. The *Creative* pattern struggles most with those who do not communicate directly. The *Creative* pattern expects everyone to be direct. In their view, such people do not tell it like it is. If an *Investigator* pattern is attempting to enroll a

*Creative* pattern, he or she will need to be uncharacteristically direct and brief. Otherwise, trust will not be established. *Creative* patterns are not generally accepting of others. Undoubtedly the *Creative* pattern will hear the message more readily from a superior with a *Creative* pattern or perhaps an *Inspirational* pattern. It really *does* matter who delivers the message.

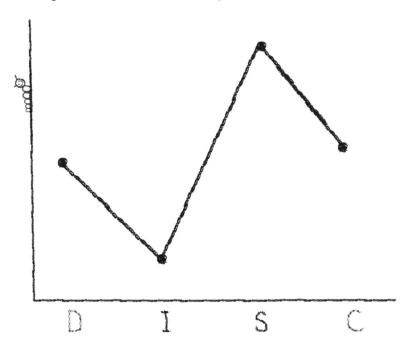

**Figure 15: Investigator Pattern DiSC Profile**

Whether you are attempting to enroll a friend in a personal change you want to undertake or persuade a board of directors to support a culture change of your entire enterprise, you will need to establish and build rapport. Neurolinguistic programming (NLP) teaches an ability to connect by establishing rapport through matching and pacing. This can be viewed as developing the skills needed to adapt in order to close the gap between your own behavioral profile and that of each enrollee. The extent of the difference in behavioral profile is one way to judge how much of a stretch it will be to have two people effectively communicate.

If the enroller is unable to establish rapport, he or she will not be able to effectively communicate and so will fail to enroll the enrollee in the change. So what is rapport? It is simply working to see the world from the other's point of view. When attempting to establish rapport with someone, it is vital that both verbal and nonverbal communications convey the same message. After all, the vast majority of communications is nonverbal. For example, if you are attempting to enroll the board of directors you would do better to dress in a similar way, use the same phrases, and adopt the same tone of voice. Fitting in is a powerful human need. It helps find the common ground upon which to base a relationship.

Sitting next to someone and adopting a very different posture is the quickest and surest way of identifying what happens when you are out of rapport. The communication is awkward. Note that it is a very bad idea to simply and quickly copy the enrollee. It looks like mimicking, and that will actually break rapport. It should be done more naturally. The intent is to slowly approximate the enrollee's posture. This matching actually occurs naturally when two people are in rapport.

Matching extends beyond posture to rhythm of movement, facial expression, rate of breathing, voice tone, tempo, and pitch. Matching is not a gimmick; it is a way to help you imagine what it is like to be the enrollee. Obviously, with an entire board of directors the best you can hope for is to match some approximation of the group to establish and maintain rapport.

This approach may appear to be manipulative. Indeed, if your real goal is at the expense of the persons or persons you are attempting to enroll, then it is manipulation. Ultimately it will fail. The purpose must be based in doing a better job of enrolling others in a change that will provide them a benefit. The best way for the enroller to appear genuine in his or her attempts to build rapport is to focus entirely on understanding the enrollee's point of view. By consistently reminding yourself that you are working to identify in what way the change benefits the enrollee, your rapport will occur more naturally.

A related way of building rapport is to match the emotional state of the person or room. In the case of our board of directors, the general emotional state of the room might be elevated, perhaps due to the previous agenda topic or perhaps because of a misinformed response to your proposed change. It is important to acknowledge the emotion and somewhat match it before pacing away to something else. Let us assume that the chairman responds to your initial outline with "That's the dumbest idea I have ever heard." You might reply, if it is true for you, with "I can understand why you would think the idea is stupid. I am really concerned that you think that." Only after it is clear from their body language that the enrollee(s) have responded to being acknowledged could you move to pace away from the emotional state. Perhaps you could say, "Could I take a few moments to explain why I think this approach will best help us achieve our goals?"

Relationship skills are a great addition to being competent, but they are no replacement for it. Even if you identify mutually satisfying goals and do a fine job of enrolling others in the change, you must then deliver, otherwise trust will break down. Once trust has broken down, the potential supporting person no longer helps you stay accountable but instead works against you to become one of your obstacles to change. No amount of rapport will compensate for not doing what you said you would do. Even then, and especially in a corporate environment, there will always be those who cannot and will not be enrolled.

So what do you do when you have tried everything and despite your best efforts there are those that are not enrolled? AUBURN had worked hard to enroll everyone in the changes to the Engineering Department. The culture shift away from the heroics that had marked its past with the professionalism that was its future was well underway. Martin prided himself in his engineering ability. He was usually called upon to fight the fire at the last moment and rescue the product development from certain failure. The new culture was so proactive that his value had shifted. But he failed to recognize the benefit of becoming the mentor for the greatly enlarged engineering team. He took his view of the world to another company where he could simply repeat the last ten years of his career.

### You're Fired!

If enrollment will not work, self-selection will often remove the obstacle. People are usually quite astute at recognizing when they no longer "fit" in a culture. But what do you do when someone is passively aggressively obstructing a change? Unless you have something of greater importance to the enrollee with which to trade, their obstructing must be somehow neutralized. That does not mean that everyone who objects to a given change must be fired. What is does mean is that if an individual refuses to enroll, even after you've made attempts to adapt to their needs and motivations, action must be taken to prevent them from becoming an insurmountable obstacle. Yet too often individuals are fired for resisting a change, and only afterward do we see that their fears and concerns were well founded. If addressed up front, these objections can help us achieve the change we are seeking. Sometimes the person who continues to find fault with the approach may only need to have his or her effect somewhat reduced until the change gets going. Perhaps a change in assignment is enough. Unfortunately what usually happens is that we simply hope they will not quietly sabotage our proposed effort to change. As difficult as it appears and only when there is truly no alternative, it is in everyone's best interest to fire the individual.

In the world of personal development, this issue frequently arises fairly quickly in any attempt to change. The usual suspects who refuse to be enrolled in such an adventure are invariably one's family or one's closest friends. Your role and the expectations that the family and friends have of the individual are even better developed than in a company. The advice from human-development teachers is always the same. They must be fired. Sounds terribly extreme, does it not, to fire your own family? The way this is accomplished is to shift the contact or communication over time so that its effect is minimized rather than completely eradicated. Over time, and once the change is a new habit, the resistance from family and friends is more manageable and normal contact can be restored, if desired.

There is a great deal to be considered when turning to our much-needed help. First we encourage friends, family, colleagues, and perhaps even the general public to hold an individual or a company accountable. We go on to build a supportive mastermind group to help break our current mind-set. Even so, there will always be resistance to a change. The effect of such resistance, however well meaning, may sabotage a change initiative, so the project must also be carefully nurtured and protected in its early stages. Then it may successfully adapt in the face of constructive resistance. We work to enroll all stakeholders in the change initiative by individually adapting the aim and the reason(s) for the change. After establishing rapport, we address every stakeholder's individual fears and motivation in a way that they can recognize the benefit the change brings them. Despite all these efforts there may be those who refuse to be enrolled. We find a way to neutralize their effect. Then we do exactly what we said we would do and implement the change. By repeating the entire process outlined to this point in the book, we can successfully shift how an individual or an enterprise is *be*ing to effect a complete transformation. We can shift our entire reality!

## Chapter Eight

# Transformation:
# Shifting Your Entire Corporate Culture

Times are changing. As individuals awaken to a
greater reality, we are part of a much larger sea
change. Our current systems and models of reality
are breaking down, and it is time for something new
to emerge. Across the board, our models for politics,
economics, religion, science, education, medicine,
and our relationship with the environment are all
showing a different landscape than just ten years ago.

—Joe Dispenza,
*Breaking the Habit of Being Yourself:*
*How to Lose Your Mind and Create a New One*

There have been phenomenal developments in brain research
in the past ten years. The field of quantum physics shows us
the impact our very thoughts and emotions can have on
our environment. Not the other way around! Contrary to
what we have thought for so long, there have been scientific
experiments that clearly demonstrate that we can change our
reality. In one very famous experiment, an electron appears
and disappears based on the position of the observer. It
literally shifts from energy to matter based on who is watching.
I appreciate that this is a considerable stretch, but consider
this: Have you noticed that what you consistently think about,
attitudes you hold, and emotions and behaviors you experience

seem to repeat themselves? We have all been in the situation where we are stuck in a rut. Though we might wish for change, we just seem to be destined to repeat the same patterns.

How many times have you personally attempted a change and thought everything through only to falter? It is because what we consciously or unconsciously think, the attitudes we demonstrate, and the emotions and behaviors we exhibit all create our reality. Our thoughts, attitudes, and emotions and behaviors are our state of *being*. Unless we can shift our whole way of *being*, we will manifest the same environment. Nothing will change. It is no different in our business enterprises. More change efforts fail than are successful. So how is it we can transform our company and be successful in our efforts to change? Suffice to say that thinking about where you want to be is not enough.

There has been much written about corporate leadership. Thought leaders are stressing the importance of leading with heart and mind. What this means is simply that it is not enough to think new thoughts and convey them to your followers. For others to follow they need to feel emotionally involved. As a leader, you must be emotionally invested in the change to be recognized as authentic. Once again it is the alignment of our entire way of *being* that yields impactful results and accomplishes the change to move us to where we want to be. In a way, transformation of the individual or the enterprise is a process of alignment.

## *Journey of Transformation*

In chapter 1 we began this journey by first becoming aware. It was likened to waking up. Our challenge is to move out of the box. In a state of victimhood we cannot be empowered to create any change. The three main routes to develop this awareness and climb out of the box were force or trauma, frustration, and finally by being inspired. Another way to consider this initial part of the journey is to consider that we are attempting to step outside of our own thoughts, attitudes, emotions, and behaviors. If we can, even momentarily, shift our way of *being*, our mind-set, then we can imagine something different.

Recall that LANDIS was a software developer facing bankruptcy. LANDIS had many others who could be held responsible for its poor health. The financial-reporting systems were being upgraded, and due to a myriad of integration issues no accounts had been produced for several months. No one really knew, or perhaps even avoided knowing, how desperate the situation was at that time. The funding for its major product development was running out and the state was unwilling to consider additional funds. The funding had disguised the serious lack of other fee-paying work. The bank was unwilling to extend the further credit that was needed to fuel any kind of growth in fee-paying work. The software product was overly ambitious and at least a year or two from commercial exploitation, so could not be relied upon to save the enterprise. But the trauma of complete failure is a very effective way of forcing a shift from victimhood to awareness.

The problem is that this effect is only fleeting. It seems unsafe to simply break all patterns and leap into the unknown. It is unsettling, and invariably we simply return to our status quo because we feel vulnerable. Awareness is a prerequisite to transformation, but it is only one part of the whole. The process of transformation is a holistic one. The same holds true for an individual as for a corporation. We move from victimhood to awareness by *being* responsible. But we can only get real about our situation if we establish and stay in a safe place where we can be vulnerable. This is where the leader or leaders of a corporation must effectively model vulnerability. They must show everyone in the company that it is okay to feel unsure. That state is a prerequisite to getting real about our situation. In effect we are looking to sustain the suspension of our thought, attitude, emotion, and behavior patterns long enough to envision something different. If we want to shift our way of *being*, we need to be clear about what we are moving away from before we create what is it we want to move toward.

Before INSOL embarked on its vision to be the world leader in safety-critical systems, it first questioned everything it was doing. For almost twenty-five years the business had grown based on the strength of a single founder. As more professional managers joined the business it started to question its structure, processes, hidden assumptions, and habits. It questioned the thoughts, attitudes, emotions, and behaviors of the whole enterprise—its way of *being*. More from frustration than anything else, the business reengineered everything and found a way to do more with 40 percent less resources. Managers made it okay to constantly question its hidden assumptions, beliefs, and many habits and to propose new ways of *doing* things. The company became very aware and very real.

In our transformation journey it is rituals that help us sustain our vulnerability, and inquiry helps us get real about our situation. We highlighted that this often exposes areas where we are not functional. One of the very first things I was asked to do at SIPTON was to lead a book club to study the work of Jim Collins in *Good to Great*. In isolation, it was a very excellent suggestion. At the time the staff turnover was in excess of 70 percent per annum. There were no job descriptions, no organizational structure, and no business processes, and the HR policies and practices were inconsistent and onerous. All of these were addressed in time, but an organization, like an individual, cannot jump several rungs of the ladder. If an enterprise is not even viable, it is necessary to first take steps to return to functionality before we work to get clear about where we are headed next.

AUTRON started with a new way of *being*. By *being* reliable they discovered many ways of demonstrating their reliability. WIZARD was clear about its means of getting to where it wanted to go—its mission. It was narrowly focused on a very fast-growing cable test equipment segment of telecommunications right as they deployed digital services on cable TV networks. LOFTON had a very ambitious vision of *being* a billion-dollar company. It took some work to develop an opening for even the possibility. At first it was discarded as unachievable. But the leader persisted. As the enterprise doubled in size in under a year, it became seen a possibility. As growth accelerated, it started to be believed.

BCCC focused on retaining their inherited set of values. Their highest value was the preservation of their tradition. Their succession plan relied almost exclusively upon internal leadership development rather than hiring senior leadership talent. Every single member of the senior management team and every potential leader attended advanced leadership-development training, and each was assigned an executive coach.

SIPTON had no unifying values, mission, or vision. But the company excelled at developing goals. Each year a single overall goal would be used to provide focus on a particular competence. Each department and groups of departments would develop department-wide goals for all members of a given department to share. Each employee would also set themselves a number of individual annual goals. Over a five-year period, the organization completely reengineered itself from a very dysfunctional command-and-control-style family business into a smooth-running operation.

AUTRON had to face a limiting belief that they were a single-product start-up company. In a few short weeks it recognized the obstacle and worked to completely overcome it to go on to become a very successful systems-design house. SIPTON had to completely drop the idea that it was a commercial real estate developer when the financial markets collapsed in 2008. Ground-up development simply stopped overnight. It quickly switched to a strategy of acquisition and revitalization to help it grow by 60 percent in three years when many competitors were either downsizing or going out of business altogether. INSOL had to challenge its belief that it was the only company that really knew how to develop safety-critical systems. Once it had challenged the hidden belief, the company acquired a competitor and accelerated its dominance of the emerging market.

A common way to provoke change is to hire an external (or internal) consultant. Every one of the examples in this book is from personal experiences. What is most interesting is that however far I had gone in my own journey seemed to exactly match what that particular enterprise needed at that time. Or so I thought.

What is most interesting about the examples in this and other chapters though is that every one of the businesses made great progress in one or more of the areas throughout the book, but none had mastered all of the elements of transformation equally well. Where one had stuck fast to its values it failed to get clear about its goals. Another that achieved functionality was never able to handle some of its obstacles. Yet another had a very clear vision and mission but never was real about its strengths and weaknesses. In all cases, none of the enterprises really became everything they could be, though every one of them would be called successful. Every one of them accomplished significant change. So why transform and why work to align all of these elements?

It is only by a more holistic view of your enterprise and your environment that you can fully transform. Otherwise we chase the management fad of the day and seek to put a patch over our problems and never achieve any lasting shift in our way of *being*. It does not last. The only way to not only achieve a shift but to sustain it is to simultaneously work on all of these elements of transformation. Some companies have already started.

## Conscious Capitalism

A number of organizations have started to look at themselves a little differently. Frankly, it is time. For too long our trust in corporations large and small has withered in the face of huge failures driven by greed and a hunger for power. We live in an increasingly global economy. We have only to look at the interconnectedness of our financial institutions. Worrying news from a very distant corner of the world wipes huge gains off our stocks. The responsibilities of these companies extend way beyond fiscal responsibility to shareholders. It is a holistic responsibility to all of their stakeholders. Instead of attempting to enforce some level of social responsibility, more enlightened companies recognize their crucial role and the interdependence of our enterprises in the global marketplace. Zappos, Whole Foods, the Container Store, and Google are *being* intrinsically trustworthy, authentic, caring, compassionate, and collaborative. Their leaders and their entire cultures strive to maintain consciousness.

## A Place to Start

So where do we start? Is there some means by which we can embark on the journey? Again, the field of personal development has something to teach us in our corporate leadership roles. Something very special happens when we are able to shift from our own state of victimhood to get at least a glimpse outside of the box. Then to avoid falling back into victimhood we are able to sustain our vulnerability, enough to get real about our situation. The means of which I speak is volunteerism. Any individual who is stuck in a rut is encouraged to serve someone less fortunate.

SIPTON's Season of Giving was very well received by all of the employees. Between Thanksgiving and the end-of-the-year holidays, each employee selects a charity of his or her choice. They have an opportunity to stand up in front of their peers and enroll others in their cause. Invariably there is a very personal reason for the choice. Tears flow. The company then makes a donation to that particular charity in the name of that employee. Now in its third year, it has become one of the highlights of the year at SIPTON.

LOFTON introduced a very different program that led to many acts of volunteerism. From a single inspiring talk, a huge servant-leadership program was launched. A specialist in servant-leadership was retained, and waves of senior executives, department leaders, and managers were exposed to the program. Each was taught the main principles of servant-leadership. Then a full 360° survey was conducted for each participant. There followed a period of intensive coaching and accountability reviews to test whether individuals were demonstrating the principles of servant-leadership. As the program grew, participants started to hold each other accountable. The effect was quite remarkable and demonstrably shifted how LOFTON was *being*. Still years later, past employees talk about the impact that servant-leadership had on them as individuals and the impact on their families and their friends. It sponsored many acts of volunteerism both inside the company and in the employees' communities.

## *Are You Ready?*

Are you ready to lead your company through transformation? Can you transform your business by simply *being* who you really are? It is my belief that you can. By first *being* you can model for others. They in turn will model for still others, until your entire enterprise shifts. You will have transformed your company into the one you always intended it to be—a conscious entity that makes a difference for others; one that provides a vehicle for meaning and contribution. I truly believe that corporations are some of the potentially most influential organizations in the world. If our corporate leaders model transformation, then our enterprises will follow. In turn, our businesses will *be* the change we would all like to see in the world. Are you up to the challenge?

> *In a world of role-playing personalities, those few people who don't project a mind-made image—and there are some even on TV, in the media, and the business world—but function from the deeper core of their* being*, those who do not attempt to appear more than they are but are simply themselves, stand out as remarkable and are the only ones who truly make a difference in this world. They are the bringers of the new consciousness. Whatever they do becomes empowered because it is in alignment with the purpose of the whole. Their influence, however, goes far beyond what they do, far beyond their function. Their mere presence—simple, natural, unassuming—has a transformational effect on whoever they come into contact with.* (Tolle, A New Earth: Awakening to Your Life's Purpose, 107, emphasis mine)

# Bibliography

Andreas, Steve. 1994. *The New Technology of Achievement.* New York: HarperCollins.

The Arbinger Institute. 2000. *Leadership and Self-Deception.* San Francisco: Berrett-Koehler.

Bradshaw, John. 2005. *Healing the Shame That Binds You: Recovery Classics Edition* (Recovery Classics). Deerfield Beach, FL: Health Communications.

Byrne, Rhonda. 2006. *The Secret.* New York: Atria Books.

Katie, Byron. 2002. *Loving What Is.* New York: Three Rivers.

Campbell Foundation. 2004. *Pathways to Bliss.* Novato, CA: New World Library.

Canfield, Jack. 2005. *The Success Principles.* New York: HarperCollins.

Cloud, Henry. 2010. *Necessary Endings: The Employees, Businesses, and Relationships That All of Us Have to Give Up in Order to Move Forward.* New York: HarperCollins.

Collins, Jim. 2001. *Good to Great.* New York: HarperCollins.

Dispenza, Joe. 2012. *Breaking the Habit of Being Yourself: How to Lose Your Mind and Create a New One.* New York: Hay House.

Friedman, Edwin H. 1999. *A Failure of Nerve: Leadership in the Age of the Quick Fix.* New York: Seabury Books.

Greenleaf, Robert K. 1970. *The Servant as Leader.* New York: Paulist Press.

Hendricks, Gay. 2009. *The Big Leap: Conquer Your Hidden Fear and Take Life to the Next Level.* New York: HarperCollins.

Kahneman, Daniel. 2011. *Thinking, Fast and Slow.* New York: Farrar, Straus and Giroux.

Kelly, Matthew. 1999. *The Rhythm of Life.* New York: Simon & Schuster.

MacPhee, Robert. 2010. *Manifesting for Non-Gurus—How to Quickly and Easily Attract Lasting Results.* Encinitas, CA: Heartset, Inc.

Marston, William Moulton. 1928. *Emotions of Normal People.* London: Keegan Paul Trench Trubner and Company.

Nasar, Sylvia. 1998. *A Beautiful Mind.* London: Faber & Faber.

Partners in Leadership. 2004. *The Oz Principle. Change the Culture, Change the Game. How Did That Happen?* New York: Penguin Group.

Patterson, Kerry, Al Switzler, Ron McMillan, and Joseph Grenny. 2011. *Crucial Conversations: Tools for Talking When Stakes Are High.* New York: McGraw-Hill Companies.

Platt, Harlan D. 1998. *Principles of Corporate Renewal.* Ann Arbor: University of Michigan Press.

Raiten-D'Antonio, Toni. 2004. *The Velveteen Principles: A Guide to Becoming Real—Hidden Wisdom from a Children's Classic.* Deerfield Beach, FL: Health Communications, Inc.

Rohn, Jim. 2013. BrainyQuote.com, Xplore Inc. Accessed April 7, 2013. http://www.brainyquote.com/quotes/quotes/j/jimrohn147498.html.

Schawbel, Dan. 2010. *Me 2.0: 4 Steps to Building Your Future.* New York: Kaplan.

Seligman, Martin E. P. 2002. *Authentic Happiness.* New York: Simon & Schuster.

Sheehy, Gail. 1974. *Passages: Predictable Crises of Adult Life.* New York: Random House.

Sheehy, Gail. 1995. *New Passages: Mapping Your Life across Time.* New York: Random House.

Tolle, Eckert. 2005. *A New Earth: Awakening to Your Life's Purpose.* London: Penguin Group.

Williams, Margery. 1922. *The Velveteen Rabbit.* New York: Delacorte Press.

# About the Author

Ron J. West is a results-focused executive coach, consultant, and speaker with a unique ability to inspire both individual and corporate transformation. Mr. West has invested his entire career in the growth and development of both individuals and companies in Europe and North America. If you ask Ron why he is so successful, he will say, "I am passionate about what I do." This passion is evident in his dedication to lifelong learning, from his formal education to his ongoing pursuit of the most innovative and effective ideas in the fields of personal and corporate transformation.

After graduating from the University of Westminster, Ron earned his master's degree from Brunel University in West London. Ron believes that his greatest strength lies in his ability to take the principles of personal transformation he's learned from the field's top practitioners and apply them to the corporate world. According to Ron, "Individuals often have trouble seeing their own strengths and weaknesses clearly. This is just as true in the world of business as it is in our personal lives. That's why people—and businesses—have trouble changing.

"My specialty is inspiring corporate leaders to recognize and remove the obstacles to their own and their companies' growth, development, and success." With his unique ability to inspire and connect with all of the stakeholders involved in businesses, Ron has been able to make a positive and lasting difference in the performance of every single corporation he's had the privilege of working with. For companies fortunate enough to discover Ron's unique blend of business acumen, insight, and integrity, the potential for success is unlimited. And that is his promise—to move you and your company from limited options to limitless possibilities.

> *"Ron inspires those that report to him with thoughtful wisdom, precise feedback, and hard truths. He manages to do all this while garnering a level of support, engagement, and action that immediately impacts the organization's bottom line. He is that good."*
> —Todd A. Uterstaedt, president and CEO, Baker & Daboll

To learn what a positive and lasting difference Ron could make to you and your company, visit ronjwest.com.

# Index

Page numbers with "*ill*" in them indicate an illustration on page.

**A**

accidents, protecting self and experiencing, 110
accountability
  buddies, 123
  change and, 121–24
  of company, 42
  using mastermind groups in, 124–26
action, need to take, 43
adapting behavior, in recruiting help, 131–36
aim and focus, turning point and, 42
alignment
  to commitment to change, 115–18
  Identity-Environment, 117*ill*
  Mission-Market, 118*ill*
  purpose and, 62–63
  to values, 89
Allied Ronin, leadership-development program by, 23–24
Amazon.com, vision of, 64

Andreas, Steve, *The New Technology of Achievement*, 93, 149
Apple, mission and vision at, 76
The Arbinger Institute, *Leadership and Self-Deception*, 27–28, 149
attachment vs. consciously inquiring, of ideas, 30–31
AUBURN
  beingness at, 69
  branding through messaging at, 122–23
  enrolling everyone in changes, 136
  using consulting firm branding tool, 38
*Authentic Happiness* (Seligman), 77, 151
authority, as precept of corporate renewal, 45
autocratic leadership, 52, 55
automatic (unconscious) habits
  learning, 5
  shifting from, 1–2

AUTRON
   beingness at, 68, 144
   consciously address reality at,
      114–15
   developing goals at, 93–94
   developing new way of
      being, 143
   gaining awareness at, 6–8
   mission and vision at, 82
   overcoming external events
      in change efforts, 105–6
   turnaround and growth of,
      48–52
   turning point of, 44
   victimization of, 14, 16
awareness
   about, xxiii, 1–2
   being responsible and, 12–14,
      17, 18
   developing rituals for, 28, 70
   driving styles exercise for
      developing sustained,
      22–23
   four stages of, 2–5
   learning unconscious
      habits, 5
   state of victimhood and,
      14–18, 141–42
   through force, 5–6
   through frustration, 9–10
   through inspiration, 10–12

**B**

balancing goals, 93–97
BCCC, retaining set of
   values, 143

*A Beautiful Mind* (movie),
   29, 150
Be-Do-Have illustration, 67*ill*
behavioral models, DiSC, 34–37,
   34*ill*, 36*ill*, 52–54
behavioral profiling, 34–39
being responsible
   shifting to state of, 17–18,
      65–66
   shifting way of being and,
      69–71
beingness
   branding and, 72–74
   vs. doingness, 66–69
*The Big Leap* (Hendricks), 98,
   109–10, 150
bliss, definition of, 78
boundaries, redefining, 57–58
Bradshaw, John, *Healing the
   Shame That Binds You*, 45,
   149
BrainyQuote.com, 151
branding
   beingness and, 72–74
   corporate vs. product, 122
*Breaking the Habit of Being
   Yourself* (Dispenza), 139, 149
breakthrough goal, 86–87
broken vs. improving, 48
burning platform, 103, 109
buy-in
   enrollment and getting,
      128–31
   as precept of corporate
      renewal, 45

Byrne, Rhonda, *The Secret*,
43, 149

## C

"call to genius," 110
Campbell, Joseph
in finding your bliss, 78
*Pathways to Bliss*, 40, 149
Canfield, Jack
*Chicken Soup for the Soul*, 14
on courage, 77
on masterminding with
people outside own
field, 120
on new kind of leadership,
xiii–xv
personal transformation
programs, xxi, 78
reestablishing safe
environment at
workshops, 25
*The Success Principles*, 14, 25,
58–59, 120, 149
on working with
accountability buddy, 123
capitalism, conscious, 145
CCL (Center for
Creative Leadership),
leadership-development
programs at, 33
Center for Creative
Leadership (CCL),
leadership-development
programs at, 33
change management
about, 115

emotional buy-in to values
in, 89
following best practices of,
99–104
change management field
getting buy-in in, 128
resistance in, 126
change of mind, glucose levels
and effecting, 69–70
*Change the Culture* (Partners in
Leadership), 121, 150
*Change the Game* (Partners in
Leadership), 121, 150
charitable giving,
transformational process of,
xxviii
*Chicken Soup for the Soul*
(Canfield), 14
Chopra, Deepak, xxi
chunking (dividing)
big picture into goals, 83–84
dreams, 81–82
group related tasks, 91–92
project into phases, 104
time frames, 89–90
Cloud, Henry, *Necessary
Endings*, 58, 149
coaching, providing on
one-to-one basis in
establishing trust, 27
cognitive dissonance, 74–75,
97, 122
collaboration, oil and gas
industry, 31
Collins, Jim, *Good to Great*, 49,
142, 149

"Come As You'll Be" party, xiv
comfort zone, getting results
in, 114
commercial real estate leader
profile, DiSC, 37*ill*, 131
communication
in change efforts, 103
establishing rapport in,
134–35
"Complete the past to embrace
the future" (Canfield success
principle #29), 58–59
conflict and stress, causes of, 110
conscious, possibilities when
courageous and, 77
conscious capitalism, 145
conscious habits, going from
unconscious to, 1–2
conscious vs. unconscious,
treatment of people, 27
consciously competent stage of
awareness, 4
consciously incompetent stage
of awareness
about, 3–4
moving from unconsciously
incompetent to, 5–12
consciously inquiring vs.
attachment, of ideas, 30–31
consulting firms
branding inquiry approach as
product, 37–38
hiring, 144
conversations, having tough, 58
corporate change, effective, xxii

corporate culture, shifting,
139–47
corporate planning, 89
corporate renewal, four precepts
of, 45
*Corporate Responsibility Officer*
(*CRO*) magazine, "100 Best
Corporate Citizens" list, xxviii
corporate sponsors, role played
in change efforts by,
100–101
corporate vs. product
branding, 122
cost/benefit, of change efforts,
108–9, 115
courageous, possibilities when
conscious and, 77
creative pattern DiSC profile,
131–33, 132*ill*
CRM (Customer-Relationship
Management) tools, 56
*CRO* (*Corporate Responsibility
Officer*) magazine, "100 Best
Corporate Citizens" list,
xxviii
Crowe, Russell, 29
*Crucial Conversations* (Patterson
et al.), 58, 150
Customer-Relationship
Management (CRM) tools, 56

**D**

daily steps approach to goals,
84–85
data and technique, obsession
with, xxii

developing vs. dysfunctional, 48, 49
DiSC behavioral model tool
commercial real estate leader profile, 37*ill*, 131
creative pattern profile, 131–33, 132*ill*
employees vs. leadership profiles, 100–101
in identifying behavioral patterns, 131
investigator pattern profile, 132, 133*ill*
open to change profile, 102*ill*
profiles of author, 52–54, 53*ill*, 54*ill*
Quadrant Behavioral Model, 34*ill*
quadrants in, 36*ill*
quantifying this leadership effect using, 34–39
resistant to change profile, 102*ill*
Dispenza, Joe, xxi
*Breaking the Habit of Being Yourself*, 139, 149
dividing (chunking)
big picture into goals, 83–84
dreams, 81–82
group related tasks, 91–92
project into phases, 104
time frames, 89–90
doingness vs. beingness, 66–69
dreams
achieving, 72
chunk (divide), 81–82

personal transformation and, xxvi
driving styles exercise, for developing sustained awareness, 22–23
"Drop out of the 'Ain't it awful club'" (Canfield success principle #25), 58
dysfunction
discovering, 39
realistic view of situations and, xxiv–xxv
dysfunctional vs. developing, 48, 49

**E**
Einstein, Albert, on solving problems, 29
emotional goals, 85
*Emotions of Normal People* (Marston), 34, 150
enabling goals, 85–86
engagement, in change efforts, 101–3
enlightenment, mastery of self and, 18
enrollment
firing people refusing, 136–37
process of, 128–31
environment, quantum physics and, 139
evolution, process natural selection of, 63
experiential training, 12–13

extension, as precept of
corporate renewal, 45
external events, in change
efforts unanticipated,
105–6, 115

**F**

*A Failure of Nerve* (Friedman),
xix, xxii–xxiii, 52, 150
"fake it until you make it," 71
feeling safe, 20–24
"Find a wing to climb under"
(Canfield success principle
#44), 59
firing people
close to you, 56–58
refusing to change, 136–37
focus and aim, turning point
and, 42
"following your bliss," 78
*Forbes* magazine, on personal
branding, 72
force (trauma), awareness
through, 5–8
forgiveness, 58–59
four precepts of corporate
renewal, 45
four stages of awareness, 2–5
Friedman, Edwin H., *A Failure
of Nerve*, xix, xxii–xxiii,
52, 150
frustration, awareness through,
9–10

**G**

Gandhi, Mahatma, on being
change, 71
Gantt charts, 90–91
gas and oil industry, idea of
collaboration in, 31
getting real
about, xxiii–xxiv, 19–20
attach sharing experiences to
ritual, 25–28
behavioral profiling, 34–39
finding safe place, 20–24
using inquiry to facilitate
shift in thinking, 28–34
GGS, developing business goals
at, 85
glucose levels, effecting change
of mind and, 69–70
goal setting, art of, xxvi–xxvii
goals
about, 80
balancing, 93–97
breakthrough, 86–87
chunk (divide) big picture
into, 83–84
commitment to change and,
113–18
daily steps approach to,
84–85
demonstrating for greater
good of, 112–13
developing corporate, 143
developing personal, 93–94
emotional, 85

enabling, 85–86
following
    change-management best
        practices, 99–104, 115
    purpose of, 81
    rapid-rehearsal technique,
        88–90
    recording intentions and, 97
    reviewing outcomes of, 112
    setting, 80–81, 84
    turning into intention,
        xxvi–xxvii
goal-seeking machine, human
    mind as, 74–75
*Good to Great* (Collins), 49,
    142, 149
gratitude, expressing, 16–17
Greenleaf, Robert K., *The
    Servant as Leader*, 150
growth
    autocratic leadership during
        periods of, 55
    style of leadership during, 51,
        52–54
    vs. turnaround, 44, 48–51
growth cycles, smoothing
    out, 83

**H**
habits
    going from unconscious to
        conscious, 1–2
    improving goals related to, 86
    learning, 43
    learning unconscious, 5

happiness, authentic, 77
have-do-be principle, 66
*Healing the Shame That Binds
    You* (Bradshaw), 45, 149
help, recruiting
    about, 120
    accountability and, 121–24
    adapting behavior in, 131–36
    enrollment process in,
        128–31
    firing people refusing to
        change, 136–37
    overcoming resistance and,
        126–28
    staying accountable using
        mastermind groups, 120,
        124–26
Hendricks, Gay, *The Big Leap*,
    98, 109–10, 150
hierarchy of needs (Maslow), 40,
    41*ill*, 44
*How Did That Happen?*
    (Partners in Leadership),
    121, 150

**I**
ideas, attachment vs. consciously
    inquiring of, 30–31
illness, protecting self with, 110
improving vs. broken, 48
in the box
    challenge of moving out of
        box, 141
    state of victimhood and
        staying, 146

treatment of people out or, 27

individual renewal, four precepts of, 45

induction training, 11

initiative fatigue, in change efforts, 107–8, 115

inquiry

DiSC behavioral model, 34–37, 34*ill*, 36*ill*, 37*ill*

exercise describing culture of company, 29–30

Katie model of, 30

Nash model of, 29

using consulting firm for, 37–38, 144

using to facilitate shift in thinking, 28–29

insight, change and, xix

INSOL

acquiring MICON, 3

branding through messaging at, 123

changing beliefs at, 144

establishing breakthrough goal at, 87

facing challenges at, 122

shifting way of being at, 142

inspiration, awareness through, 10–12

intention, turning goals into, xxvi–xxvii

intentions

achieving, 113–18

recording, 97

investigator pattern DiSC profile, 132, 133*ill*

**K**

Kahneman, Daniel, *Thinking, Fast and Slow*, 69–70, 150

Katie, Byron, xxi

*Loving What Is*, 30, 149

Kelly, Matthew, *The Rhythm of Life*, 150

knowing self, 18

**L**

LANDIS

shifting from victimhood to awareness, 141

turnaround and growth of, 48–50

language, introducing new phrases during growth and development, 51

Lao-tzu, *Tao Te Ching*, 1

law of attraction, 43

leadership

DiSC profiles of employees and, 100–101

essence of, 82, 97

during growth of company, 52–54

modeling vulnerability, 142

during turnaround style of, 51

*Leadership and Self-Deception* (The Arbinger Institute), 27–28, 149

leadership-development
  programs
  by Allied Ronin, 23–24
  at CCL, 33
learned skills and natural
  talents, strengths as, 77–78
letting go, process of, 16–17
linguistics field, inquiry exercise
  in, 32–33
list of values, being captured on,
  71, 73*ill*, 74
LOFTON
  balancing goals at, 95
  building momentum in
    organization, 84
  communication in change
    efforts at, 103
  habits and unconscious
    behaviors of, 4
  improving goals related to
    habits at, 86
  initiative fatigue at, 107–8
  major automation project at,
    126–27
  modeling leadership at, 97
  realistic view of, xxiv–xxv
  servant-leadership initiative
    at, 26–27, 146
  smoothing out growth cycles
    at, 83
  style of leadership during
    growth at, 53
  unwelcomed feedback at, 127
  vision of, 143
*Loving What Is* (Katie), 30, 149

**M**

MacPhee, Robert, *Manifesting
  for Non-Gurus*, 113–14, 150
*Manifesting for Non-Gurus*
  (MacPhee), 113–14, 150
manipulation, 135
Marston, William Moulton
  DiSC behavioral model,
    34–37
  *Emotions of Normal People*,
    34, 150
Maslow, Abraham, hierarchy of
  needs, 40, 41*ill*, 44
mastermind groups, staying
  accountable using, 120,
  124–26
mastery of self, enlightenment
  and, 18
matrix management, 86
*Me 2.0* (Schawbel), 72, 151
meaningful change,
  instituting, 43
MICON, INSOL acquiring, 3
midlife passage, 53, 61
mind-made image, projecting,
  147
mind-mapping tool, using for
  developing vision, 83
mission
  about, 63
  Be-Do-Have illustration, 67*ill*
  discussing, 82
  of Starbucks, 64
  vision and, xxv–xxvi, 65–66,
    74–79

of WIZARD, 143
modeling others, 81–82, 97
"moments of being," 60
money, talking about, 51

**N**

Nasar, Sylvia, *A Beautiful Mind*, 150
Nash, John, 29
natural selection, process of evolution by, 63
natural talents and learned skills, strengths as, 77–78
*Necessary Endings* (Cloud), 58, 149
Neurolinguistic Programming (NLP)
  ability to connect in, 133–34
  about, 93
  overcoming unconscious sabotage, 111
  rapid-rehearsal technique, 88–90
*A New Earth* (Tolle), 49, 147, 151
*New Passages* (Sheehy), 61, 151
*The New Technology of Achievement* (Andreas), 93, 149

**O**

obstacles to change efforts, removing
  about, xxvii, 98–99
  alignment and, 115–18, 117*ill*, 118*ill*

commitment to change and, 113–18
demonstrating change is for greater good, 111–13
following change-management best practices, 99–104, 115
identifying unconscious saboteur, 109–11, 115
initiative fatigue, 107–8, 115
insufficient worth in of change effort, 108–9, 115
overcoming external events, 105–6, 115
overcoming unexpected side effects, 106–7
oil and gas industry, idea of collaboration in, 31
"100 Best Corporate Citizens" list (*CRO*), xxviii
out of box
  challenge of moving, 141
  shifting state of victimhood getting, 146
  treatment of people in or, 27
outcomes, reviewing goal, 112
*The Oz Principle* (Partners in Leadership), 121, 150

**P**

Partners in Leadership, books in Oz series, 121, 150
*Passages* (Sheehy), 60, 61, 151
*Pathways to Bliss* (Campbell Foundation), 40, 149

Patterson, Kerry, *Crucial Conversations*, 58, 150
personal branding, beingness and, 72–74
personal development field accountability in, 123
balancing goals in, 94–95
consolidating what is learned, 108
firing people refusing to change in, 137
imagining achieving goals in, 82
modeling others in, 81–82, 97
SMART goals in, 95–96
volunteerism in, 145–46
personal transformation choices in, 113
dreams and, xxvi
support systems in, xxvii–xxviii
using inquiry to facilitate shift in thinking, 28–34
personal-transformation workshops
about, xxv
experiential, 12–13
PERT charts, 90–91, 91*ill*
Peters, Tom, on personal branding, 72
phrases, introducing during growth and development new, 51
planning
benefits of, xxvii
corporate, 89

for unexpected, 90–93
unfolding plans, 92–93
Platt, Harlan D., *Principles of Corporate Renewal*, 45, 150
precepts of corporate/individual renewal and, 45
preservation, state of, 44
*Principles of Corporate Renewal* (Platt), 45, 150
product vs. corporate branding, 122
project-management methodologies, 83, 89, 90–93
projects, nurturing, 127
purpose
about, xxv–xxvi, 60–62
mission, vision and, 65–66, 74–79
ultimate, 62–63

**Q**
quadrant behavioral model, DiSC, 34–37, 34*ill*, 36*ill*
Quadrant Behavioral Model, DiSC, 34–37, 34*ill*, 36*ill*
quantum physics, environment and, 139

**R**
Raiten-D'Antonio, Toni, *The Velveteen Principles*, 28, 151
rapid-rehearsal technique, 88–90
rapport, establishing, 134–35

real estate leader profile,
    commercial, DiSC, 37*ill*, 131
recovery
    growth, development and,
        49–50
    stay in mode of, 44
    twelve-step program and,
        45–47
recruiting help
    about, 120
    accountability and, 121–24
    adapting behavior in, 131–36
    enrollment process in,
        128–31
    firing people refusing to
        change, 136–37
    overcoming resistance and,
        126–28
    staying accountable using
        mastermind groups, 120,
        124–26
relationship skills, 135
relationships
    causes of problems in, 110
    planning and, xxvii
removing obstacles, about, xxvii
resistance, overcoming, 126–28
resourcing, in change
    efforts, 101
responsibility, taking, 12–14,
    17–18, 65–66
reviewing outcomes, of
    goals, 112
*The Rhythm of Life* (Kelly), 150
risking unpopularity, leaders, 52

rituals
    attach sharing experiences to,
        25–28
    developing awareness
        through, 28, 70
    safe environments and, 25–26
    sustaining vulnerability, 142
Rohn, Jim
    BrainyQuote.com, 151
    on goals, 80

**S**

sabotage of change efforts,
    overcoming
    about, 98–99
    alignment and, 115–18, 117*ill*,
        118*ill*
    commitment to change and,
        113–18
    demonstrating change is for
        greater good, 111–13
    following
        change-management best
        practices, 99–104, 115
    identifying unconscious,
        109–11, 115
    initiative fatigue, 107–8, 115
    insufficient worth in of
        change effort, 108–9, 115
    overcoming external events,
        105–6, 115
    overcoming unexpected side
        effects, 106–7
safe place
    building, 20–24, 42

rituals and creating, 25–26
Samurai warrior,
    leadership-development
    game, 23–24
Schawbel, Dan
    *Me 2.0*, 72, 151
    on personal branding, 72
*The Secret* (Byrne), 43, 149
self-fulfilling prophecy, 113–14
Seligman, Martin E. P., *Authentic*
    *Happiness*, 77, 151
sense of purpose
    about, xxv–xxvi, 60–62
    mission, vision and, 65–66,
        74–79
    ultimate, 62–63
*The Servant as Leader*
    (Greenleaf), 150
servant-leadership initiatives,
    26–27, 146
Sheehy, Gail
    *New Passages*, 61, 151
    *Passages*, 60, 61, 151
shifting way of being,
    55–60, 142
side effects, overcoming in
    change efforts unexpected,
    106–7
SIPTON
    accountability and change
        at, 121
    annual goal-setting process
        at, 83–84
    being professional vs.
        professionalism, 66

corporate learning and
    employee turnover,
    108–9
culture modeled on
    leadership, 100–101
developing goals at, 143
dysfunction and development
    at, 49, 142
gaining awareness at, 9–10
identifying behavioral
    patterns using DiSC
    behavioral model tool
    at, 131
identifying corporate brand
    at, 74
Season of Giving
    initiative, 146
transformation at, 90
SMART goals, 95–96
social networks, personal
    branding and, 73
software engineering service
    work, 48
Starbucks, mission, vision, and
    value statement of, 64
state of mind, being as, 68
"stop" process exercise, 43
strengths, as natural talents and
    learned skills, 77–78
stress and conflict, causes of, 110
*The Success Principles*
    (Canfield), 14, 25, 58–59,
    120, 149
support systems, in personal
    transformation, xxvii–xxviii

survival, going beyond
    about, 40–43
    changing leadership style,
        51–54
    needing to shift, 55–59
    turnaround and growth, 44,
        48–51
    turning point and, 42, 43–47
survival mode
    at turning point, 56
    willingness to accommodate
        change in, 42
systems, 31

**T**

tasks, grouping related, 91–92
teaching others, 78
teams, with shared purpose,
    62–63
technique and data, obsession
    with, xxii
Thatcher, Margaret, 6
*Thinking, Fast and Slow*
    (Kahneman), 69–70, 150
Tolle, Eckhart, xxi
    *A New Earth*, 49, 147, 151
Townsend, Dale, xxi, 9–10
toxic people, avoiding, 58–59
training, induction, 11
transformation
    about, xxviii
    committing to, xxi–xxiii
    shifting corporate culture,
        139–47
    using planning process in,
        89–90

trauma (force), awareness
    through, 5–8
trust
    exercise on, 10
    provide coaching on
        one-to-one basis in
        establishing, 27
turnaround
    four precepts of corporate/
        individual renewal
        and, 45
    vs. growth, 44, 48–51
    style of leadership during, 51,
        55–56
Turnaround Management
    Association, 45
turning point
    getting to, 42, 43–47
    shifting way of being at,
        55–60
twelve-step program, 45–47

**U**

unconscious habits, learning, 5
unconscious saboteur, in change
    efforts, 109–11, 115
unconscious vs. conscious,
    treatment of people, 27
unconsciously competent stage
    of awareness, 5
unconsciously incompetent
    stage of awareness
    about, 3
    moving to consciously
        incompetent, 5–12

underpinning, in change efforts, 104

upper limit switch, tripping, 110

**V**

values
about, 63–64
Be-Do-Have illustration, 67*ill*
creating way of being using, 71, 74
generating emotional buy-in to, 89
list of values, 71, 73*ill*, 74
retaining set of, 143
shifting, 67–68
of Starbucks, 64
starting with, 65
*The Velveteen Principles* (Raiten-D'Antonio), 28, 151
*The Velveteen Rabbit* (Williams), 19, 151
victim cycle, 121
victimhood, state of
awareness and, 14–18, 141–42
shifting, 146
victimized, being, 13–14
vision
about, 63
of Amazon.com, 64
Be-Do-Have illustration, 67*ill*
discussing, 82
of LOFTON, 143
mission and, xxv–xxvi, 65–66, 74–79

as precept of corporate renewal, 45
of Starbucks, 64
tools for developing, 83–87
visualizations, "stop" process, 43
volunteerism
servant-leadership initiative, 146
transformational process of, xxviii, 146
vulnerability
leadership modeling, 142
rituals sustaining, 142

**W**

way of being
creating, 71–72
developing new, 143
shifting, 142
ways of being
branding and, 72–74
example, 73*ill*
Williams, Margery, *The Velveteen Rabbit*, 19, 151
Williamson, Marianne, xxi
willpower to make changes, 42, 45
WIZARD
beingness at, 69
mission of, 143
transformation of engineering department in, 4
Woolf, Virginia, 60

**Z**

Zarvos, Jim, xxi

CPSIA information can be obtained
at www.ICGtesting.com
Printed in the USA
LVHW02*1610310818
588551LV00001B/1/P